Henry Albert Stimson

Questions of Modern Inquiry

A series of discussions

Henry Albert Stimson

Questions of Modern Inquiry
A series of discussions

ISBN/EAN: 9783337063757

Printed in Europe, USA, Canada, Australia, Japan

Cover: Foto ©ninafisch / pixelio.de

More available books at **www.hansebooks.com**

QUESTIONS OF MODERN INQUIRY

A Series of Discussions

BY

HENRY A. STIMSON, D. D.

PASTOR OF THE BROADWAY TABERNACLE CONGREGATIONAL CHURCH
NEW YORK CITY

FLEMING H. REVELL COMPANY

NEW YORK   CHICAGO   TORONTO

Publishers of Evangelical Literature

" So if the tempter should persuade such a man to doubt whether the gospel be true, or be God's Word, this believer may have recourse into his soul for a testimony of it; thence he can tell the tempter by experience that he hath found the promises of this gospel made good to him. ' Christ hath there promised to send His Spirit into the souls of His people, and so He hath done by me; He hath promised to give light to men that sit in darkness, and to guide their feet into the ways of peace; to bind up the broken-hearted and set at liberty the captives; and all this He hath fulfilled upon me: all that He hath spoken about the power of His Word and grace, and the nature of its effects, I have found upon myself. The help which He promised in temptations, the hearing of prayer, the relief in distress—all these I have found performed; and therefore I know that the gospel is true.'" RICHARD BAXTER, Works, vol. xx., p. 162.

PREFACE

THESE discussions are a series of Sunday evening addresses in response to inquiries that came to me suggesting the needs of my congregation. They were delivered without notes, and without thought of their publication. I have pleasant testimony that they have been helpful to some who have heard them, and I gladly and gratefully yield to the request to write them out from the stenographer's notes and furnish them to the printer. The notes were not complete, and not equally full upon all the addresses; but I have thought better to leave the addresses as little changed as possible, that they might retain the flavor and character of their original delivery.

Their only claim to attention is not any novelty of fact or argument, but that they present in a somewhat simple and compact form truth familiar to Christian students. I think I may say that they may be accepted as representing upon the various subjects discussed the position taken to-day by intelligent Christians. My aim has been in each instance so to state the truth as to make it both intelligible and acceptable to earnest inquirers. Of course my one purpose has been to lead men to an immediate acceptance of Christ —a purpose which, with deep gratitude to God, I can say was, at least in some instances, attained.

As the book is not for scholars in theology, it has not seemed well to load it with notes. I had freshly read, in particular, Bruce's " Kingdom of God "; Principal Fairbairn's " City of God," and his " Religion in Modern Life "; Liddon's " University Sermons," and his " Elements of Religion "; J. M. Wilson's " Essays and Addresses"; Matheson's " Messages of the Old Religions "; Ladd's " What is the Bible ?"; Boyd Carpenter's " Bampton Lectures "; Cave's " Inspiration of the Old Testament" ; Horton's " Verbum Dei," and Joseph Parker's reply, " None Like It"; and Professor Stearns's most helpful " The Evidence of Christian Experience"; and I went into the pulpit from time to time full of the thoughts they gave me. I desire to make grateful acknowledgment here, though the circumstances of pulpit utterance do not give opportunity for more than occasional reference in connection with some single sentence which has fixed itself in the mind. It has not seemed to me important, since delivery, to return to the various authors to mark the exact extent of my obligations.

It should be said that these addresses were delivered in connection with a musical service carefully arranged with reference to the particular theme, and so well rendered as to prepare the minds of the hearers for an impression which otherwise might not have been made. For this service I desire to express my obligations to Mr. C. B. Hawley, the accomplished musical director of our church. Quotations from the Bible, except in one address where the Revised Version was of necessity used, are made from the Authorized Version, as being the more familiar.

If the little book may prove helpful to any who are yet undecided as to the claims of Christ, my hope, and the hope of those who requested its publication, will be rewarded. With that prayer I send it on its way.

H. A. S.

" Individuals, indeed, may rescue their faith by retreating before doubt into the citadel of the soul; but the church has no right to pursue this course: so certainly as it is its duty to seek to possess Christianity as a whole, so certainly must it overcome the enemy in a true manner. It must not, indeed, allow its faith to wait on scientific demonstration, but neither can it consent to bear about discordant elements in its existence. Were it to consent thereto its faith would no longer be accompanied by an honest and good conscience; the object of its faith would become to it an imagination of its own invention."

DORNER, " Person of Christ," vol. v., pp. 71, 72.

" The temptation of this age is to try to find a middle path between faith and unbelief; to say that ' there is much to be said upon both sides '; to think that all things must be uncertain in themselves because many of the persons around us are at sea as to all things, as if they thought all things to be in a whirl because they seemed so to our neighbors who had dizzied themselves; to be browbeaten out of belief; to shrink from avowing a steadfast adherence to that which must be old because it is eternal, and which must be unchangeable because it is truth; to pick up something out of revelation which, it thinks, will not be gainsaid, and to relegate all else to be matter of opinion."

PUSEY, " Daniel," p. 452.

CONTENTS

" On the greatest points of all—those which relate to the character and attributes of God—the Bible is not only supreme, it is unique. The believer in the Bible has no need to exaggerate; he has but to state the facts as they are."

SANDAY, " Inspiration," p. 167.

" The language of the Bible grows more harmoniously luminous with the growing light. When its words are read and interpreted simply, as words still living, they are found to give the spiritual message which each age requires, the one message made audible to each hearer in the language wherein he was born."

WESTCOTT, " Revelation of the Father," p. 8.

" We do not at all know everything which we have Luther and the Reformation to thank for. We have become free from the spirit of narrowness; we have, because of our progressive culture, become capable of returning to the source and apprehending Christianity in its purity. We have regained the courage to stand with firm feet on God's own earth, and to feel within us our human nature God-endowed. Let spiritual culture continue ever to advance, let the natural sciences grow ever broader and deeper, and the human spirit enlarge itself as it will, yet beyond the majesty and moral culture which shines and lightens in the Gospels it will not advance."

GOETHE, in Fairbairn, " Religion in History," p. 64.

I

THE ATTITUDE OF CHRISTIANITY TOWARD INQUIRERS

" When people are really in earnest it may be better sometimes to leave them alone, instead of calling the poor, honest seekers hard names which the speakers themselves don't understand."

CHARLES KINGSLEY, " Yeast," p. 138.

" To give all men liberty to judge for themselves, and to expect at the same time that they shall be of the preacher's mind, is such a scheme of magnanimity as one would scarcely imagine any one would be weak enough to devise in speculation, and much less that any could prove hardy enough to avow and propose to practise."

DODWELL, " Freedom of Thought."

" It is easy for those who are content to live on like the rest of the world to be orthodox. They believe what was believed before them, and never trouble themselves with testing it. But when a soul is anxious about the truth, and would deal with it as with a precious jewel, then things are not quite so easy. How wrong is it, then, to rush upon just such sensitive souls, to cross-question and to gag and stun them, when we ought, on the contrary, to give them liberty of speech, that they may gain confidence and suffer themselves to be led aright!"

BENGEL, in Dorner, " History of Protestant Doctrine,"
vol. ii., pp. 228, 229.

14

QUESTIONS OF MODERN INQUIRY

I

THE ATTITUDE OF CHRISTIANITY TOWARD INQUIRERS

In beginning a series of addresses which have to do with questions that are occupying the public mind, it is not my purpose to preach a sermon. I desire rather to speak in the simplest terms possible, and as nearly as may be as a friend would talk to a friend on matters of grave concern.

Our opening question must be, What is the attitude which Christianity assumes toward inquirers? We shall aim to get quickly upon common ground as preliminary to all subsequent discussion.

People may, perhaps, be roughly divided into three classes. There are those whose minds are settled, and practically closed, as to the question of religion. They have accepted it once for all. They know what they believe. It satisfies them.

They need no corroborative proof, and they do not wish to be disturbed. A lawyer past middle life, intelligent and successful, said to me the other day: " I have no interest in these controversies. I settled the question of religion long ago. I cannot be perpetually going over those things anew." It is hard for such a man to understand the difficulties that confront other minds, or to see the use of discussion. It is not strange that he thinks that discussing doubts spreads doubt.

Then there are those whose minds are made up against Christianity, either as it is or as they think it is. They will not willingly read or hear anything in its favor.

Between these two classes there is the large class of those whose minds are open to the truth, but who are continually disturbed. They are not wholly convinced. Many of them are sustained in a conventional attitude of respect toward religion, or even of belief in it: they are far from being unbelievers; they are not at all prepared to break with the past, or with the faith and practices of their friends; but they are not at peace.

This is a condition arising from very varied causes. With some we may regard it as largely constitutional: their minds are peculiarly hospitable to doubt; they interrogate everything. Others feel the lack of the knowledge necessary to settle these questions which come from one side

and another. The air is full of them; they drift
upon us from the magazines and newspapers and
the idle talk of the dinner-table. A young lady
came to me the other day in serious distress. A
friend had told her of a book he had seen, "representing in colors all the different fragments of
which the Bible had been composed, and it looked
like a crazy-quilt." He was going to get her a copy,
and she did not know what to believe. One may
smile at her perturbation, but it was serious, and
differed from that in the minds of very many only
in that it was outspoken. It may coexist with
a gracious and beautiful life, and with a faithful
performance of all religious duties. But in sensitive souls, under the pressure of helplessness and
fear, it breeds a feeling of hypocrisy which is in-
tolerable, or it dries up the springs of a joyous
and growing faith until personal religion becomes
merely a perfunctory service or a tradition.

Doubts, to-day, appertain to far more than the
make-up of the Bible. They apply even to the
existence and character of God, the nature of
inspiration, the future life, the very philosophy of
religion, and, perhaps most of all, to the worth
of the life Christians live, as measured by what
they profess. And in all these directions they
are obstacles, great and serious, in the way of not
a few who, we may believe, are anxious to find
the truth and God.

First of all, then, I want to call your attention to this: that Christianity makes its demand upon every mind on the ground that its claims are both catholic and authoritative. Christianity is not the faith of any race, or of any class within a race. It is a religion for everybody. In this respect it is separated from all other forms of faith the world has seen. It has no narrow, limited truth to present; all that it possesses in its consciousness of a revelation from God it offers to the whole world, presenting this to every man, with the knowledge that the only limitation that exists will be found in the man himself—in his capacity for the truth, and in his readiness to receive and apply it. It holds that all men are in need of it. No man is in any such exceptional position as to have reason to hide his doubts or to be ashamed of them, still less to think that they are insuperable. Christianity welcomes them. It anticipates them. It pledges itself to remove them. It must do so, or it cannot be the universal faith it proclaims itself.

For a similar reason the claims of Christianity are authoritative. Because its truth is for all men, its duties are for all men. It presents itself as coming from God, and as the voice of God; it addresses men, whether as individuals or families or communities or races, as always and everywhere owing allegiance and service to God.

This claim of Christianity must be accepted, or Christianity has no claim to be accepted. It is often admitted that religion is excellent, is valuable in the home and in society ; its laws are to be regarded, its ceremonies observed, its doctrines promulgated, for the good they do. But Christianity never presents itself on these prudential grounds. These are wholly incidental and secondary. Its message to every man is authoritative. "Give me thine heart" is a divine command no less than a divine invitation. God's right to the whole man is the fundamental fact.

It is also to be observed that Christianity makes its appeal always and everywhere on the ground of the truth. It does not appeal to any opinion about the truth, or to any feeling that the truth may produce or has produced, still less to any superstition. It rests its claims upon truth, and truth as understood in its ordinary acceptance— that is, facts open to examination and capable of being proved day by day and hour by hour. You of course are familiar with the emphasis our Lord · lays upon this; but it may be well to turn to the testimony of a single Gospel. Take John's, for example : "The Word was made flesh, and dwelt among us, full of grace and truth;" "For the law was given by Moses, but grace and truth came by Jesus Christ;" "My record is true;" "Ye shall know the truth, and the truth shall make

you free;" " Ye seek to kill Me, a man that hath
told you the truth;" " I am the way, and the
truth, and the life;" " When He, the Spirit of
truth, is come, He will guide you into all truth;"
" Father, sanctify them through Thy truth: Thy
word is truth;" " For this cause came I into the
world, that I should bear witness unto the truth.
Every one that is of the truth heareth My voice."

This, then, is the attitude which Christianity
takes toward every inquiring mind. It stands
before us, offering the truth; and with the truth
it offers evidence. For historical facts it offers
historical testimony; for facts of the personal
experience it offers internal evidence; but it always appeals to the man through the intellect.
It recognizes man as a thinking being, capable of
exercising judgment and choice; capable of knowing the truth and being moved by it. It has full
knowledge of man's nature. It knows what lies
back of the intellect, and does not fall into the
mistake of appealing only to the intellect; but it
comes as a reasonable faith, offering itself to
reasonable minds.

Another characteristic of Christianity in approaching men of inquiring mind is that it presents a book—the Bible; but it presents it as a
help, rather than as an authority. It offers the
book as a testimony and as a record.

There are many theories about the book, both

as to its character and its origin. But Christianity requires no acceptance of these theories. Indeed, it requires in advance no acceptance of the statements of the Bible itself. It believes those statements; it holds them authoritative for its own faith and practice; but it imposes them upon no inquirer. It says simply, "Here is the book. Read it, and let it tell its own story." We know what this book has done in the past in helping burdened and sinful men; we know what it can do now. There are other books of prime value— books which have been read by successive generations; but no other book can hope to find the acceptance which the Bible has found for its vitalizing power. This we know. We ask you, with or without any opinion about it, just to try it. With so much of receptive mind as you can command, suffer it to speak to you for itself concerning your own deepest needs and sorest difficulties. The world has never outgrown it. It has proved itself immensely wise and immensely comprehensive; it will be sure to prove itself helpful to you.

Furthermore, Christianity presents to inquirers this book as a record of the progress of truth in the past. It says, "Here is the record." All other records give small fragments of that story, and those so imperfectly that no one can be sure that he is reading aright. Outside the Bible there is no record of man's progress toward God. Here, however, is the story of the process by which the chosen race advanced step by step under divine guidance, from the days of Abraham to the days of Isaiah; from a condition of knowledge of God as when one gropes in the darkness, to thoughts of God so full, so large, so sufficient, that we read them to-day feeling them unparalleled by anything the modern world has produced.

The story of that long development is found in this book. Christianity stands with the book in its hand because it believes itself the product of that process. God has thus fitted the world for Himself; and Christianity appeals to men to-day from the standpoint to which the world has come. It is a present-day religion with a history. It is that up to which the centuries have led.

The Bible tells the tale, furnishing the record of the progress and the sure ground for the present faith. Now, because of this, the church requires no acceptance of the Bible in advance. It does not say that you must believe that Adam and Eve were in a garden by the river Euphrates, or that Balaam's ass spoke, or that the earth was drowned in a great flood, or that Jonah was swallowed by a whale. It does not ask that you shall accept these or any other single statement. What does it ask? It asks that you accept the book as a trustworthy friend, and not as a fraud

or an impostor; that you shall have reverence for
it as a book that has saved life—not physical life,
but lives that shall live on through all eternity.
It asks that you open it reverently and hear what
it has to say to you. We shall all be content
when it is allowed to bear its own testimony and
has produced its own effect. The church's confidence in regard to the Bible is that the Bible
will justify itself. It needs neither your defense
nor mine; and as for doctrines in regard to it,
and theories, they have changed with the years,
but the Bible remains unchanged.

Now you see that religion, or the church, or
Christianity—use which term you will—demands
simply those things which it has a right to demand. It demands that a man shall be serious,
because the issues with which Christianity deals
are the greatest with which we can concern ourselves. It has a right, therefore, to demand that
a man shall be in earnest. Thomas, you remember, did not believe that the Saviour had risen.
Why? He was not there to see. He did not
have evidence he might have had, therefore he
did not believe. Now the Saviour had a right
to require that Thomas should believe. He said
to him, therefore, " Reach hither thy hand, and
thrust it into My side." So Christianity demands, and believes it has a right to demand,
that a man shall face his doubts, and not ignore

them or remain helplessly overcome by them. It demands that he shall sit down quietly and read the Bible for himself, feeling assured that if he does it will accomplish in him what it has accomplished in countless hearts before.

Thomas thought he needed peculiar testimony ; but there is no intimation that when the opportunity was given he did put even his finger upon the Saviour's wounds.　Conviction and faith had come to him already.　That has been the process ever since.

If you are in earnest, if you believe that there are in your life possibilities of good and of evil which are daily contending for mastery, and that you are being carried where you would not simply because you delay, then Christianity has a right to demand that you decide.　There is nothing noble or noteworthy in doubt.　It is simply ignorance and indecision.　The church is set in the world to compel men to take sides in reference to Jesus Christ.　That is the whole object of its preaching and its testimony.　It stands as a witness to the love of God which has made it possible for men to be His sons.　It believes men will hear and obey, but they shall not remain indifferent.　" Choose ye this day " has been its message from the beginning.　The utter unreason of unbelief is set forth in the Saviour's words to the Jews: " And if I say the truth, why do ye

not believe me?" We shall all be judged at
last on the ground of the truth which God has
given to us in the revelation of His Son, in whom
we might have believed if we would, and who,
had we believed, would have led us every one,
no matter what our sins or our fears or our per-
plexities, to the Light.

II

WHAT AM I TO THINK ABOUT GOD?

" Earth's crammed with heaven,
 And every common bush afire with God;
 But only he who sees takes off his shoes;
 The rest sit round it, and pluck blackberries."
                MRS. BROWNING, "Aurora Leigh," bk. vii.

" Philosophy is based on the affirmation of God's existence,
and not upon the denial of it."
                FISKE, " Cosmic Philosophy," vol. ii., p. 377.

" It is easy for any one in the cloisters of the schools to indulge himself in idle speculations on the merits of works to justify
men; but when he comes into the presence of God he must bid
farewell to these amusements, for there the business is transacted
with seriousness. To this point must our attention be directed
if we wish to make any useful inquiry concerning righteousness:
how we can answer the celestial Judge when He shall call us to
account. Let us place that Judge before our eyes, not according
to the inadequate imaginations of our minds, but according to
the descriptons given of Him in the Scriptures, which represent
Him as one whose refulgence eclipses the stars, whose purity
makes all things appear polluted, and who searches the inmost
soul of His creatures; let us conceive of the Judge of all the
earth, and every one must present himself as a criminal before
Him, and voluntarily prostrate and humble himself in deep solici-
tude concerning his absolution."
                CALVIN, " Institutes," vol. iii., p. 12.

28

II

WHAT AM I TO THINK ABOUT GOD?

THROUGH many a long year the Psalms have answered this question with the personal testimony of men who had come to know God each for himself. The loving-kindness and tender mercies of God are a blessed reality, and as an actual experience have taught many an inquiring mind what to think about God, in a surer and fuller way than any argument can do. But unfortunately there are those who, because of doubts suggested to them from without, or by reason of their conscious weakness before temptation, fail to interpret God's dealings with them, and despair of ever gaining such personal knowledge of Him as will enable them to trust Him as their Saviour.

The Bible was originally written by men who believed in God, for men who believed in God; now many come to it with such preliminary unbelief that it fails to address them. For some the authority of the church has been sufficient; it has dispelled doubt and given peace. There have

29

been times when the absolute inerrancy of the
Scriptures was unquestioned, and the written
Word was the end of controversy; but there are
multitudes who find it no easier to accept an infallible book than an infallible church. Therefore
every one of us who finds his heart stirred by the
ancient Psalms, and who delights to "call upon
his soul and all that is within him to bless His
holy name," is also bound to turn to his friends
and neighbors, and at least try to give a reason
for the faith that is in him.   It ought to be entirely possible for us all to-day to answer such
inquiries as "Where shall I find God?" and
"What am I to believe about God?"

The human mind being what it is, we ought
not to find it difficult to discover a common
starting-point.   There are some things we all
know to be true.   We are conscious of our own
existence: we all can say, "I am."   Every man
realizes, also, that this "I am" is a personal
reality.   The skull is a box containing a curious
mechanism.   Hidden somewhere within dwells
the person I, myself.   Our thought is so organized that we cannot rest content with the consciousness of this fact.   We must reach out beyond ourselves.   Doing this, we come to other
beings like ourselves, all equally able to say,
"I am."   From them, in turn, our mind reaches
farther into the infinite universe to find some

being who is not, like ourselves, limited and finite. The spirit of man always does this and always has done it. We are at times oblivious of this experience; but in our better moments we are aware that there is in us all a longing to find this Being who possesses infinite wisdom and unlimited resources. Our conception of existence is incomplete without Him. We find ourselves dependent—strangely so—and that in many directions. And we do not escape from the feeling; advancing years, with increase of knowledge or of prowess, only widen the sphere, and strengthen the conviction that we are insufficient of ourselves. We long to know One who is not dependent—that is, God. We can stifle this feeling, we can for a time escape from it, but it is there, the common possession. The hour is sure to come when, sooner or later, each will know himself as one

> " Swimming at night alone upon the sea,
> Whose lesser life falls from him, and the dream
> Is broken which has held him unaware;
> And with a shudder he feels his naked soul
> In the great black world face to face with God."

Or, to take another line of thought, we discover within our hearts—we need not define just where—a feeling which we call the sense of obligation or accountability. We say, " I ought."

Oh, the hidden power of that word! We awake
to it, and we believe that all men in all conditions
are under its dominion. " It is right to do right."
Who can question it? Explain this discovery as
you will, it is there, permanently in your heart.

When, recognizing this, a man begins to ask,
" What ought I to do?" he finds his thought at
once reaching out beyond himself. He discovers
his accountability. His thought turns his face
upward. He finds that this sense of " ought," or
accountability, is not satisfied when his thought
rests upon his neighbor, for his neighbor is like
himself. There is that within which reaches into
the infinite realms above, which cannot rest until
it gathers to itself the conception of the holy God.
I ought, I am accountable, I owe obligations, because there is the All-good somewhere ; and not
only somewhere, but here. I am in His presence.
He is beneath me ; He is before me ; He is above
me. " Whither shall I flee from Thy presence?
If I ascend up into heaven, Thou art there : if I
make my bed in hell, behold, Thou art there. If
I take the wings of the morning, and dwell in
the uttermost parts of the sea ; even there shall
Thy hand lead me, and Thy right hand shall hold
me."

Thus, along the lines of our necessary thought,
we come to the one conclusion. We do not absolutely prove the existence of God, but we prove

the necessity of God. There must be this Being to whom we recognize our obligation; who is himself the All-good, the supreme object of our love, the final reward of our service.

Starting, then, with this preliminary conception, as we look out into the world we find everywhere curious suggestion of an artificer, a fashioning hand in nature. As Agassiz said, "Atoms look like manufactured articles." Some men talk about a "carpenter-God," as if the Christian's idea is that God came with a set of tools and made the universe and man.

Nature did not make itself; that is certain. A letter has been recently published in which Charles Darwin wrote to Asa Gray, the botanist, of a certain orchid, "Does this look as if done at a single accidental stroke?" To this Dr. Gray replied, "No. Does it look as if done by many?" No multiplication of the number of blind chances or of the impacts of molecules will account either for the orchid or for man.

Whichever way we look we find everywhere in nature the suggestion of adaptation of means to ends. Not to-day, not yesterday, but in all the development of the world, in the parts as in the whole, God's hand is seen, God's thought is revealed. Professor Dana's last word in closing his "Geology" is, *Deus fecit*—"God made it." That record, it is true, is written differently from other records, but it is written everywhere in nature for those who can read. As Carlyle puts it, " The Infinite is more sure than any other fact, but only men can discern it."

Quite as clear is God's hand in human history. Can any one believe that the fortuitous collision of molecules has been the ultimate cause there? Life is certainly something more than a wild dance of human atoms, like motes in a sunbeam. Can any one doubt that there was a divine providence in Marathon and Salamis, or in the outcome of the long struggle between Rome and Carthage? Did God have nothing to do with the smiting of the Arabs by Charles Martel at Tours, and the consequent turning back of the Saracen invasion of western Europe? Was it an accident that the empire of Charles and of Philip, behind which was the Inquisition and the Roman Catholicism of the sixteenth century, should grind itself to pieces in vain struggle with the handful of men who in the marshes of Holland were set to save Protestantism and the modern world? Or was the fate of the Spanish Armada a splendid chance?

Who prepared the way for Columbus, and led him from the East Indies to the West, and then apportioned his discoveries so that North America should unwittingly be left open to settlement from northern Europe? Who guided the Pilgrims, and uprooted the French, and finally drove out the English and made America free? Has there been no divine Hand in all this?

And this is only the outside of history. Suppose we had time to look within, what strange providences we should find in the preparation that lies back of all these great events! Everywhere man has had free play, yet everywhere we can see the guiding Hand. There has been a long struggle for civilization and liberty and knowledge and something of righteousness and truth, with many a defeat, and often what seemed to be doom. But what progress there has been! How wonderful is the human story! Inexplicable in itself, a veritable "crazy-quilt" when spread out, but to-day to be seen oriented to Jesus Christ, all from beginning to end relational to Him. He is the key to it all. Ancient history led up to Him. He came, and at once the world began to unfold from Him.

Thus asking, "What shall we think about God?" we arrive always at the same result. He is a personal God; One who has responded to our thoughts; whose will has furnished the law for our wills; whose intelligence is to be read in all His wondrous works in the world that lies about us. Call Him by what name you will—Jehovah, God, the Heavenly Father—it is always the same conception: the One from whom man comes,

under whom and in whom man lives, and to
whom we owe that accountability which is the
fundamental fact in man's life.

It only remains to bring this conception of God
to the test of its effect upon the men who hold
it.   We must go to the Bible for the record.   It
is the story of a people whose conceptions were
immature and, if you will, childlike; but we find
them holding to their conception of one personal
and holy God, and advancing under its influence,
until both their conceptions of God and righteousness and truth, and the literature in which these
conceptions are preserved, are the grandest the
world has known.   The Israelites, under the influence of these views, were the only people of
all antiquity who advanced steadily to what the
world now accepts as the true idea of God.   We
possess hymns sung on the Nile four thousand
years ago, many ancient writings of the Assyrians,
noble thoughts of Confucius, and lofty aspirations
in the Vedas; but where is to be found one of them
furnishing the theme and the setting of a great
musical composition, or entering as a vitalizing
conception into modern worship or life?   Every
oratorio, every great anthem, is set to the words
of the Bible.   Here alone is discovered an undy-
ing energy; here alone are thoughts of God and
man, of eternity and holiness, which, though old,
are ever new; here is a literature so lofty in

thought, so stately in expression, and through all
so sane and so simple, that it constitutes a world
of its own.   Nowhere else is to be found a permanent faith in a personal God, and nowhere else
is to be found a record of life like this.   Israel
has been the one fruitful source of the religious
and moral development of the world.

We know God to-day not only as no sages of the
Orient ever have known Him, but even as Israel
herself did not know Him ; because, superadded to
all Israel had, we have the revelation of the New
Testament.   Then, when you ask a Christian to-
day, " What am I to think about God ? " the answer is at once on his lips : " We are to think of
God as Jesus Christ, our Saviour and our Friend."
He cannot fail to say, " I will mention the loving-
kindnesses of my God."   The all-righteous, the
all-pure, the all-wise, the all-powerful, holy God,
the Maker of the heavens and the earth, has had
compassion on me.   He has sought me and found
me.   He has spoken to my heart.   He has answered my prayer.   I am nothing—less than
nothing—for I am sinful; but He has come to
me, and has given me something of His spirit to
live in my soul ; He has accepted me, with all my
failures and limitations, with all my consciousness
of sin and weakness, as a tribute and a witness to
Himself.   And now what I, by God's grace, have
been led to think and know about God is what

God, through me His messenger, would have you, His child and my brother, think about Him.   Accept Him, trust Him, love Him ; commit the keeping of your soul to Him, because you are His child, and He is your Father which is in heaven.

III

WHAT AM I TO THINK ABOUT THE BIBLE?

.

"Of all ancient literatures, of all ancient writings possessed by man, the writings with the largest sense of humanity, the greatest sense of the rights of the individual, the noblest conception of labor and its reward, of society and its function, are the writings of the Hebrews. . . . In a word, the ideas that make men of you run back into the belief in God and God's law that came through Moses."

FAIRBAIRN, "Religion in History," pp. 138, 140.

"The Bible has been the Magna Charta of the poor and of the oppressed; down to modern times no state has had a constitution in which the interests of the people are so largely taken into account, in which the duties, so much more than the privileges, of rulers are insisted upon, as that drawn up for Israel in Deuteronomy and Leviticus; nowhere is the fundamental truth that the welfare of the state, in the long run, depends upon the uprightness of the citizen so strongly laid down."

HUXLEY, in Sanday, "Inspiration," p. 181.

"The more I read the Bible, without almost any thought of questions of inspiration, but simply as a record of fact, of precept and principle, of judgment and of mercy, of God's acts and ways (i.e., the principles of His acts), all culminating in Christ, as a revelation of what God is to man and what man was created to be to God, the more my whole moral being responds to it as being a revelation of God. The authority of the Bible is to me supreme, because it commands my reason and conscience. I feel it is from God. It was once otherwise with me. It is so no more, and the older I get the more my spirit says 'Amen' to it."

NORMAN MACLEOD, "Life," vol. ii., p. 316.

III

WHAT AM I TO THINK ABOUT THE BIBLE?

I DO not propose to add another to the many statements of doctrine concerning the Bible as the Word of God. There are too many already —i.e., if you chance to be curious for proof. But I propose to offer you the book itself, and simply to lead you along a line of thought in regard to it which may enable you to settle for yourself what you are to think about the Bible.

Here, then, is the book. It is stamped " The Bible." That word comes to us through the Latin from the Greek. The Greek neuter plural was transferred into Latin as a feminine noun, *Biblia*, the Book. It really meant " the books," or " the writings." The Bible was also called at first *Bibliotheca*, the Sacred Writings. This declares the real nature of the volume. It is a collection of documents—a book only in this sense.

On the title-page of many of our Bibles you find the statement that it was translated into English by the authority of King James in the year 1611, certain learned men being invited by the king to come together for the purpose. We know that this was not the first attempt at an English Bible, but it had the advantage of being generally regarded as the best, and as such gained wide and permanent acceptance. It was translated from such Greek texts as were then extant.

We have to-day a revision of this our English Bible, published in 1885. The reason for the revision, as you all know, is the fact that since 1611 nearly all the more important ancient manuscripts have been discovered, including one or two complete ones of the New Testament as old as the fourth century; and scholars have studied and collated these with a minuteness and care which give us a text probably more nearly correct than any that has existed since the original writings disappeared. The revision of the English translation in the light of a better text was committed, by act of the Convocation of the Province of Canterbury, in February, 1870, to two companies of approved biblical scholars—one for the Old and one for the New Testament—in coöperation with two similar American companies. As a result we have the book before us, the Bible in its latest and most perfect form.

We open it, asking, "What does it say of itself?" It says, indeed, very little. Here at the end is a writing called the Revelation, bearing the name of the Apostle John. It says he was commanded to write the things which he had seen—things which certainly no other man ever saw, and in connection with which the command would most naturally occur. The Apostle Peter, in a brief epistle, says that "men spake from God, being moved by the Holy Ghost"; and the natural supposition is that if some were moved to speak, they or others were also moved to write. The Epistle to the Hebrews opens with the statement: "God, having of old time spoken unto the fathers in the prophets by divers portions and in divers manners, hath at the end of these days spoken unto us in His Son." In an Epistle of Paul to Timothy we find these words: "Every scripture inspired of God is also profitable for teaching, for reproof, for correction, for instruction which is in righteousness." There is little said beyond these more or less indirect statements. Yet there is one luminous passage in the Gospel of Luke. He explains his writing as follows: "Forasmuch as many have taken in hand to draw up a narrative concerning those matters which have been fulfilled among us, even as they delivered them unto us, which from the beginning were eye-witnesses and ministers of the Word, it seemed good to me also, having traced the course of all things accurately from the first, to write unto thee in order, most excellent Theophilus; that thou mightest know the certainty concerning the things wherein thou wast instructed." He had been a contemporary and in part an eye-witness of these events, so he felt called upon to sit down and write the narrative of them in the spirit of a careful and painstaking historian. He lays claim to so much of credibility.

This is not all the Bible has to say about itself. It says God's hand was in the work, but it does not say how it was in it. It speaks just as we should if we should try to tell a friend some of the things that have happened to us. The writers are often conscious that " the burden of the Lord " is upon them, and that they " have the mind of Christ "; but they are never careful to describe in what this appears, or to define its effect upon their manner of writing. When they are delivering a message they say so. It is enough for our purpose to say that they regarded themselves as simple and credible historians, or direct and truthful utterers of the thought that was committed to them.

Looking further, we discover a gap between the Old Testament and the New of several centuries. The later writings of the Old Testament have much to say about the future, and One who is to come; and this is the theme with which the New Testament begins. The New Testament is, indeed, simply the unfolding of the truth up to which the Old Testament has led—the story of the Coming One ; His birth, His life, His teachings, His death and resurrection, with an interpretation of their significance. So that in the New Testament we have a small library, the work of different hands writing in the years immediately following the death of Jesus, and having this as its definite purpose, to tell His story. Some of the books bear the names of their authors. We know very little of most of them. Matthew was a tax-collector, Luke a physician, Paul a scholar and by trade a tent-maker, the others fishermen. Though it seems little doubtful, the authorship of Acts has long been in dispute. In regard to Hebrews, Origen said, in the third century, " Who wrote the Epistle to the Hebrews is known only to the Lord."

These writings, which with but slight modification or questioning have in their entirety been received through all the Christian centuries, have been the single means of disseminating the revelation and doing the work of God in the Lord Jesus Christ. They have been the object of incessant attack by the enemies of Christ from the first century until the present day. They have borne the brunt of the battle against the Christian church. If they were spurious they would have been quickly disposed of, for that has been invariably the fate of spurious writings on matters of any importance; but through the centuries the books in this little collection have proved their authenticity and genuineness by the test they have stood—both are established beyond reasonable dispute. They are not forgeries; they were written at the time and under the circumstances claimed for them; they have from the beginning been in circulation as the trustworthy and authoritative statement of the truths which they declare. So much for the New Testament.

In the Old Testament we find a somewhat different state of things. The Old Testament is translated from the Hebrew. It contains a larger number of documents than the New, covering a far longer period both of authorship and of history. Some of the writings are confessedly composite: various sources of history are quoted; there are occasional bits of poetry; there are heroic songs; there are royal decrees, as in Ezra, Nehemiah, and Daniel; there are long genealogical tables, and definite compilations, as of the Proverbs. The Book of the Psalms is simply a hymn-book in five parts. Many of the books are found to be anonymous. No one knows, for example, who wrote Esther, Job, Ecclesiastes, Daniel, and, indeed, many others. They all bear distinctive names, but, except in the case of the prophets, little or no stress is laid upon their authorship.

The language in which they are written is singularly uniform, considering the long period of time they cover. There is occasional introduction of words that are Aramaic and Chaldaic —languages akin to the Hebrew—but there is very little change from first to last; the earliest are, if not purer and statelier, in every way worthy of fellowship with the latest.

As we begin to read we find them steadily moving onward from the beginning to the end. They are under one dominant purpose. No matter who wrote them, no matter when they were collected, they are parts of a whole; they lead up to a definite point; they are the story of the way in which a certain people prepared a setting for the work Jesus of Nazareth was to do; they lead straight up to Christ.

But there is much else in these old books aside from the preparation for the coming of a Saviour. We open at Genesis. Here, in the first chapter, is an account of the creation. With a few grand and rapid details of creation as the work of God, it leads up to the institution of the Sabbath. As we read it we might imagine that it was composed, as some assert, to authenticate the special holiness of that day.

We proceed to examine its detached statements. Do these accord with science? The question is natural—perhaps inevitable—but not at all as important as is made to appear. We know a great deal more about the manner of the creation—meaning by that the process by which the world was prepared for man—than any men in the past have known. Most of what is accepted now as science was born in our day. The science of our fathers was largely ignorance. Some one asks, " Does our knowledge correspond with the knowledge of the man who wrote the first chapter of Genesis?" He did not know all that we know—far from it; but he knew wonderful things. He knew that there was a beginning to creation; he knew that life came in orderly and progressive stages; and he knew—what some men do not know to-day—that man is the crown of creation, the child of the Author of all; that for him all these things were made, and in him they are to find their explanation and their purpose. He knew, furthermore, that God was in it all, and there was from the beginning a plan of God with this as its conclusion. Many men to-day, with all their science, have not grasped these truths.

What do we care whether in their lesser details his broad statements minutely correspond with the geology and biology of to-day? They tell the great story in as graphic a way as it could be told ; and they tell it truthfully—that is unquestionable—and as it is told nowhere else since the world began. Suppose it appears—which is by

no means certain—that the writer of that chapter
thought that the world as he saw it—the beneficent arena for the unfolding of the life of man
the child of God, the finished work of his own
Heavenly Father, the divinely ordered home for
his own God-enswathed life—was made in six
days of twenty-four hours each; what of it? He
knew and recorded for all time the great facts.
Is his knowledge to be belittled because it had
limitations? Think of the enlightenment it has
been to the world from that day to this. Search
the literature of antiquity for a chapter for one
instant comparable to this.

We turn to the second chapter, and find important additions to the story, if, indeed, it is not
the substance of the same story told in a different way. Man is placed on the earth under most
favorable conditions. A garden is prepared for
him. He has a fit companion. He is made to
know that what God wants is character, and that
if he has right character he shall live. Now some
man asks, "Was that an apple?" What difference does it make? The temptation was real; the
fact and its consequences are indisputable. Suppose we admit that the details are too brief, or
given in a form we cannot fully explain. "Did
snakes walk on their tails in those days?" The
narrative does not say they did. That incident
of the serpent we cannot explain. It is too brief,

and our knowledge is too incomplete. We know
nothing of the possible relations of the animal
world with the powers of evil.   Here is a story
of profoundest import, told in language the most
graphic.   It is strikingly akin to our own experience.   It holds attention to-day no less effectually than when it was written.   It declares that
man was blessed by being surrounded at the beginning with everything that heart could desire,
and that he recklessly threw himself out of that
position.   It was done under temptation essentially the same as that he encounters to-day.
The consequences were prompt and permanent.
But the arms of God's love were at once thrown
around him, and redemptive influences set immediately at work.   Then follows the long story,
through Genesis, Exodus, and the rest, of the
guidance and preparation of Israel for the coming
of the Saviour in whom that unfailing purpose of
redemption was at last accomplished.

The story, in its beginnings, was passed on
from father to son.   It gradually became the
possession of the people in whom, more or less
consciously to themselves, it was advancing for
the ultimate blessing of the world.   In time
Moses appeared.   He was the man by whom
God chose to gather up the details and fix them
in something of a permanent form.   Then comes
Samuel, and then David, and many another, each

forwarding the result and adding something to
the record. At last, after the exile, and after
several earlier efforts in the same direction, Israel
proceeds to separate these her peculiar possession
from all other writings, until they are brought
into the form in which they were when Christ
came. Then He takes them up and begins to
quote from them. "Search the Scriptures"—
your own sacred writings. They have come
down to you from the fathers; and "they are
they which testify of Me." Does He say, " Search
them that you may get knowledge of mineralogy
or zoölogy or astronomy"? No; search them
for the divine knowledge. And the men who
were taught of Christ proceed to quote them as
being the authoritative voice of God to men on
this matter of a personal religious faith and duty.

Henry Martyn's argument was certainly a fair
one. He once sat, the story goes, discussing
with a group of Persian scholars about the rela-
tive merits of the Koran and the Bible. They
were intelligent men—more astute, indeed, than
himself—and with wide information. He listened
patiently, admitting all they said in favor of the
Koran. Then he replied: "Here are some sixty-
six books. Nobody knows who wrote many of
them. They cover a period of not less than fifteen
hundred years. Manifestly no one mind could
have planned them, and no group of men, and no

nation or church. How, then, are they to be accounted for? Here is the book. It is the story of Christianity. There is but one explanation. God did it. Through all those years His heart was set unchangeably upon redeeming the world. This is the story of the process, and a chief agency in it. Set the book alongside the best you have, and tell me which should be your guide?"

Of course there are many questions for scholars to settle. We have learned much of late, but we still know comparatively little of the ancient world. All the knowledge we gain throws wonderful light upon the Bible. It has already cleared up many difficulties. There are many still unsolved. Those of to-day are not those of yesterday. Search for answers as hard as you will; only remember that the validity of the book does not turn on your answers. The great truths are settled; the purpose of God is clear; the life is there awaiting you, if you will have it.

A word in closing. God might have written a book Himself. With a pen or a graver He could have written the words on paper or stone. Some people are tempted to say that the Bible was written essentially in this way. Perhaps God ought so to have written it. The fact is that the book was not God's main purpose. What was God's purpose? Life! The book is a mere instrument. Far in the past God started a plan of

life—redemptive life—coming down to us like a
great river. It is a strong, full stream from
Abraham to Paul and John; and from them on
to us. From time to time the current threw up
to the surface various writings, and as the current
passed along these were joined one to the other,
thus forming accretions of writings. At last, in
God's good time, they were recognized as having
a special character and use, being in a measure
distinct from the stream that produced them;
filled, indeed, with its life, but presenting the life
in a peculiar and definite form. So the Bible, in
the form in which we have it, became the possession of the church, and a chief instrument in making the church what it is. In other words, the
Christian community was moved, as it believes,
by the Spirit of God, to collect the writings into
permanent and final form; and then, as so collected, the writings became the ultimate law of
the Christian community. God's purpose was
with the river; as He used men to make that, so
He used men to make the Bible, which embodies
so much of its life.

And God always uses men being what they
are—Samuel, David, Isaiah, being themselves;
consequently each man's writing is his, and not
another's. The life of Israel was very limited;
but as the centuries rolled on, the life from God
was ever deepening and widening it. So it has

come down to us. Therefore we say the Bible is God's book. No other is like it; no other has its history.

"Is the Bible inerrant?" Certainly not. Did man ever do anything that was altogether free from error? And there never has been a day, from the time the first line was written, when man has not been in some way at work upon the Bible. "Is the Bible infallible?" Certainly not, if you mean, "Is there no possibility of misstatement?" "Are there mistakes in the Bible?" Possibly; but it is singularly exact so far as we are able to test it. In the lapse of years it has been so often vindicated, even in its minuter features, that he is a bold man who to-day sets himself squarely in opposition to its statements. But it nowhere lays claim to such inerrancy or infallibility, and those claims may be left to take care of themselves. "But were not the original writings absolutely correct?" If so, God seems to have set small value upon that fact, as He suffered them so soon to be lost.

What, then, is the Bible to us? It is God's own book, because it has been God's voice to men through all these centuries; and it is infinitely better than any other voice we can listen to. God is with us always; but it is hard for us to interpret His voice in nature, much more in His providences; always hard surely to know His will.

Where, then, can we get this knowledge? In the Bible. There He speaks unmistakably. Even a child can understand it, while the wisest man finds there wisdom infinitely larger than his own. The Bible, therefore, is the way of life to him who will follow it, and the word of life to every man who longs to hear it.

IV

WHY NOT GIVE UP MIRACLES?

" This too is probable, according to that saying of Agathon :
' It is a part of probability that many improbable things will hap-
pen.' " ARISTOTLE, " Poetics."

" Miracles are not, as the old apologetics taught, divine cre-
dentials attached externally to the revelation for its authentication.
They are a part of the revelation itself. They are not violations
of the laws of nature, but events which cannot be accounted for
by physical forces or human agencies, and which therefore are
ascribed to a higher Cause. They are not known as miracles
simply by the power manifested in them—that would not distin-
guish them from the miracles of evil beings—but by their manifestation of God's grace in redemption."

STEARNS, " Present-day Theology," p. 50.

" The only question is whether we are to expect miracles at
the present time ; and this question is answered in the negative,
not through any doubt of God's ability—which is abundantly attested by the regenerative and sanctifying exercise of power to-
day—but on the ground that the redemptive revelation is once for
all in the world, and that the outward evidences of divine power
which once were necessary are no longer requisite—a consideration which passes from presumption into proof when we examine the alleged miracles of our own day, and find in them nothing
that cannot be explained as the result of God's providence. . . .
What we discover here is not our Lord manifesting God's love
in the sphere of outward nature, and doing it with that divine
economy which was intended to guard against the abuse of the
miraculous, but men invoking the miraculous for their own selfish
ends, turning the Christian church away from its distinctively
spiritual work, and endeavoring to transform it into an eleemosy-
nary institution for the healing of all diseased bodies."

STEARNS, " The Evidence of Christian Experience,"
pp. 333, 335.

IV

WHY NOT GIVE UP MIRACLES?

THE question of miracles is recognized as lying close to the center of the Christian position. Skeptics sneer at them, and inquirers find them a stumbling-block; while believers become uncomfortable when they are made the subject of discussion. Meanwhile it is plain that they are woven so thoroughly into the gospel story that they cannot be taken out without destroying it; and the Saviour himself staked everything upon them, as in his message to John the Baptist: " Go your way and tell John what things ye have seen and heard; how that the blind see, the lame walk, the lepers are cleansed, the deaf hear, the dead are raised;" and in his farewell appeal to his disciples: " Believe me for the very works' sake."

The question is not as to merely apparent miracles, such as ice to the king of Siam, or Nikola Tesla playing unharmed with electricity of two hundred thousand voltage, or the latest cure of the "metaphysical healer," or a fresh "miracle" from Lourdes. Our concern is with the miracles of the New Testament. Are they possible? Did they occur? If Hume's position is correct, that no evidence will suffice to give credibility to a miracle, then we should cease to speak of them as such, or at least we should admit that they would not be so called had they occurred to-day.

The New Testament miracles are a series of events the direct result of supernatural powers put within the control of certain persons for the purpose of arresting attention to them and authenticating their claims and words. Can we believe them to have occurred?—that is the question before us.

The notable thing in nature is that we are surrounded by forces arranged in an ascending series, in which each higher force dominates a lower one, and comes in, when it appears, with something of an element of surprise. A grain of earth is swept into the river and carried along by the mechanical force of the stream. It is dissolved, and sucked up by a rootlet, to become an element in the leaf of a tree, yielding to a chemical and a vital force. Another force appears in the browsing animal that crops and eats the leaf; and still another in the man who kills the animal. The lower forces persist, but in each case the higher supersedes them. The question is, Is there any force higher than these; any coming from outside nature and yet capable of acting within nature? "Nature" —the word—is, you remember, from the Latin

nascor, and means "the begotten, the born, the
evolved"; can that which brought it into being
still act within it, and if so can it appear and be
recognized?

It is apparent that nature is to-day in consid-
erable disorder. The face of nature, at least, is
roughly disturbed, as the result of man's wrong-
doing. Witness, for example, the effect of human
vice and crime, as it appears, not in the devasta-
tion of war, but in the condition of man's own
body. See the long and bitter struggle he has
for existence, contending with the feebleness with
which he begins life and the heredity of disease
he finds in his system. Everything seems to con-
spire against a successful issue of the contest. The
selfishness of his fellows, their greed, lusts, hates,
ambitions, combine with the entail of evil that
has come down from the past, if not to destroy
him, at least to take possession of him and add
him as another to the forces of destruction in
nature. We do not need revelation to inform us
that this is the consequence of sin. On all sides we
find evidence not only that sin to-day is universal,
but that it has been, if not from the beginning, at
least for a very long period—so long that the earth
itself bears enduring and startling record of it.

It certainly is reasonable to expect that God
will at some time deliver the earth from this
dominion of evil; it is not incredible that there

should be evidence of a redemptive process already at work. Indeed, this is most reasonable
if there is a God, and the earth is not a self-con-
stituted and self-perpetuating machine. It is not
necessary to assume that God is a " tinkerer of the
world," or to say with Theodore Parker, " There
is no whim in God, and therefore no miracle in
nature." It is enough to hold that God is not un-
mindful of the world, not inhuman. He has at
heart, and always has had at heart, the welfare
of his creatures. The Christian, because he
believes in God, believes that he has planned redemption from the beginning; therefore if miracles play an important part in the scheme of redemption, there is not only no presumption against
them, but there is every reason to expect that they
will occur when they are needed.

What, then, is the evidence that they have occurred? The way is certainly open to receive it.

Here are four ancient writings of unquestioned
authenticity. They never have been questioned
by any one worthy of attention. They are as credible as any ancient writing in existence; as credible as any ancient writing need be. They are
Paul's letters to the Romans, Corinthians, and
Galatians. Their author, the Apostle Paul, was
an intelligent man of exceptionally fine character
—the kind of man who is to be believed as telling
the truth, or at least what he believes to be the

truth. We find that in these letters he refers frequently to miracles—" signs, and wonders, and
mighty deeds "—that were wrought by him and
others, and were incidentally accepted by him and
them as connected with the work he was called to
do and the words he was commissioned to speak.
Many of these deeds—which he speaks of in the
most matter-of-fact way, as if they were so evi-
dent and so numerous that they could not be questioned—we have no means of testing. They were
the direct action of mind on mind, or of mind on
matter. But some of them we can test, and all
are so closely connected that they stand or fall
together. It cannot be questioned that spiritual
forces of unusual power emanated from Paul.
They are proved by the tremendous changes
wrought in the individuals and communities with
which he came in contact. Indeed, they are forces
which, through his writings, continue to this day.
These forces may well be called miraculous—that
is, these events are not produced by anything dis-
coverable in nature. New men are made to-day,
in all that pertains to life and character, just as
they were made then—by the power that went
forth from the Apostle Paul.

But we must go a step further. We have to
observe Paul's relation to Jesus. Paul is very
careful to say that this power which he possessed
did not originate with him, nor was he taught it.

He received it as a gift from Jesus Christ. He
says, indeed, it was the result of Jesus' being in
him. On this point, at least, Paul is to be believed.
If he possessed extraordinary powers, what more
natural than that he should have claimed for himself the full credit of them? On the contrary, he
claims only secondary possession.

What Paul, then, had, Jesus had in a still higher
degree. Jesus must certainly have spoken words
as rare as Paul's. Jesus must have wrought deeds
as wonderful. When we find Paul, therefore,
staking both his life and his teachings upon the
greatest of all miracles, the resurrection of Jesus
from the dead, beyond the credibility of Paul
under such circumstances as a witness is the
probability of the event, as that probability arises
in the character and life of Jesus. It is exactly
what we should expect. The life is to-day here;
we can handle it and see. Its story is told by
credible witnesses. It goes back to Jesus of
Nazareth. In its fullness it was in him. What
more natural than that he should work miracles,
when they were needed to bear witness to him,
or that he should give like power to chosen disciples? What more certain than that such as he
should not be at last subject to death?

This, of course, is not a line of argument original with me. It is the common and natural one
on the lips of the thoughtful believer. It does

not prove that Paul's miracles, or even those of
Jesus, were divine, you say.   No, that, perhaps,
we cannot prove; but they are the result of a
power that resembles the action of the human
spirit in its noblest movement, and they infinitely
surpass it.   A fair inference, then, is that it is the
power of God.

This, then, is to be said of the New Testament
miracles :

1. They are reasonable.   They are what we
should expect.   Natural forces are about us in
ascending series, leading up to the human will.
That is a force in nature, but altogether unique.
It seems to stand on the confines of the unknown,
prophetic of what is beyond.   These New Testament miracles are the acts of a noble nature, like
Paul's, in its noblest, its most exalted condition,
when it is open to the incoming of the world beyond.   In still higher form they appear in him
who is the Christ of God.

2. They are restorative of nature.   They are
invariably beneficent, and they do not discredit
nature.   In this sense they are no superseding or
tinkering of nature.   They are simply the inter-
vening of the hand of the Author of nature to
further the end for which nature exists.

3. They authenticate and advance the work of
redemption.   Of this there cannot be question.
If Jesus Christ came into the world to save sinners,

then his rising from the dead, and incidentally his working of innumerable beneficent miracles, were important, if not indispensable, factors in his task. They are the natural and, indeed, the inevitable expression of himself. And thus revealing him as he is, and as otherwise he could not be known, they make it vastly easier for men to believe in him. It is idle, therefore, for any to assert that miracles—meaning the New Testament miracles —are an incumbrance to Christianity, or to imply that either the Christian faith or the New Testament can be delivered from them. Paul stated the truth for all time when he said, " If Christ be not risen, then is our preaching vain, and your faith is also vain. Yea, and we are found false witnesses of God." And this the greatest of the miracles attests the others.

Thus we are crowded back to this as the final form of the question: Do you believe that God is in his world? Do you recognize him? Do you seek his miraculous aid to undo the effect of sin in your own soul? The two conclusive statements are: " Except a man be born again, he cannot see the kingdom of God," and " He that hath not the Son of God hath not life." I would convince you of the truth of the miracles because I would persuade you that the saving of your own soul is a miracle which the Lord Jesus Christ stands at this hour ready and waiting to perform.

V

THE STORY OF JESUS

" When I trace the unaffected majesty which runs through the life of Jesus, and see him never falling below his sublime claims amid poverty and scorn and in his last agony, I have a feeling of the reality of his character which I cannot express. I feel that the Jewish carpenter could no more have conceived and sustained this character under motives of imposture than an infant's arm could repeat the deeds of Hercules, or his unawakened intellect comprehend and rival the matchless works of genius."

FÉLIX, in Liddon, " Bampton Lectures," p. 195.

" How a Jewish rabbi of philanthropic mind and somewhat Socratic morals, with a few miracles, or, at least, what others took for such, and the ability to utter a few gnomes and parables; how One who was this and nothing more, and who, were he only this, were not fit to stand before Moses or Mohammed, could have caused such an effect as a new religion and church—to be able to conceive how this were possible one must first take leave of his senses."

SCHLEIERMACHER, in Fairbairn, " Theology," p. 231.

V

THE STORY OF JESUS

WHAT, in a few words, are the facts about Jesus, and what evidence is there for them? A letter has come to me asking whether there is reason to believe that there ever was such a person, and whether the story of Jesus is not a myth like many others.

Here are four documents called the Gospels. They were certainly extant as early as the year 150 A.D. Hostile criticism has been crowded back by indisputable evidence; compelled to yield decade after decade until it admits this. They must all, therefore, have been written considerably before that time in order to have gained general acceptance. There is strong evidence that at least three of the four were written much earlier. In any case they all bring us within one hundred years of the life they describe. That is, they may in this respect properly be compared with such lives of Washington as are in our hands to-day. Is there any serious difficulty in accepting these, or in estimating the facts they record?

Does not all the world, so far as these lives of Washington are read, know the main outlines of his story, and place him correctly? Would there be any reason in talking of the "Washington myth"? Or, with the histories now extant carefully preserved, is it conceivable that, say two thousand years hence, he would become mythical? Yet the case is hardly a fair parallel. No one is in antipathy to Washington, or finds any gain in discrediting him; but there has not been a day since Jesus lived when the bitterest enmity has not been arrayed against him, doing all in its power to overthrow his influence and create doubt as to his career. In every century, almost in every decade, of all this period his story has been the subject of the most strenuous and hostile criticism. Could a myth arise under such conditions? If the original narratives hold their ground; if faith in him is not only not discredited, but, on the contrary, has rapidly and steadily spread, until, in the face of every opposition, and carrying with it the requirement of fundamental reform in society and in individual lives, to-day it extends around the earth, and has come to be the very warp and woof of civilization, is it not reasonable to ask of any man that he cease caviling, and open his mind freely to see what these narratives tell us in detail about Jesus Christ?

The date of his birth is fixed with sufficient

accuracy. It was in the reign of the Roman emperor Augustus Cæsar, Herod the Great being king in Judea. There are reasons for fixing the year as the fifth before the beginning of our current chronology. His ostensible parents (for the narratives are at one in describing his birth as miraculous) were obscure Jewish peasants, though of the genealogy of David. Their home was Nazareth, in central Palestine, though he was born in their ancestral town of Bethlehem, to which, under a decree of the emperor, they had gone to be registered in the imperial census.

The conditions of his birth were not unlike those of many a famous man—Martin Luther's, for example, the miner's son in Eisleben. The difference appears in the attending events. His relatives, who were also plain people, were strangely moved. Neighboring shepherds on the hills of Judea had visions, and came to the town to tell his parents and friends what they had seen and heard. And certain strangers, of the class of soothsayers or astrologers, soon appeared coming from a distance, bringing notable gifts and doing reverence, impelled by some mysterious intimations they had received. Their coming, in connection with certain prophecies of the Old Testament, attracted so much attention that Herod, fearing the effect upon the Jews, and having ambitions for establishing his own line in succession at Jerusalem, sent to Bethlehem and secured the murder of all the male infants born there about that time, whose number could not have been large. Jesus escaped only through his parents' timely flight into Egypt.

In connection with the announcement of the angels to the shepherds occurs a word destined to become a future title of the child—the word "Saviour." It is a Greek term of such dignity that, according to Cicero, the Latin had no single term to convey it. *Salvator* was afterward introduced for the purpose. It implies a power of extraordinary and supernatural intervention, and is used to indicate One who delivers from evils too great for men to deliver themselves.

There are certain other intimations, given in a prophetic way, of the great importance of the event that has happened, but silence ensues for twelve years; then a remarkable incident occurs. His parents, having in the meantime reëstablished their home in Nazareth, go up with their son to the Passover at Jerusalem. On their return they miss him, and going back to the city find him in the temple, in a group gathered, according to the Jewish custom, about some scribes who are expounding the Old Testament law. Instead of being taught, to the amazement of all he is teaching, revealing an understanding and insight far beyond his years. His only comment in reply to his troubled parents is that he is " about his Father's business."

The important fact is that up to this hour he has given apparently no intimation of his true character and mission. He has lived a natural child's life, so that his parents thought him with the other children in the traveling company. He has shown no assumption or pretense, and has apparently laid no claim to extraordinary gifts. He was simply a child like the others. Even now he sets up no claims. He makes no attempt to overthrow the existing order, or to reorganize the world. Whatever may be revolving in his mind, he seems to have entire confidence in the ultimate power of the new life. He can wait for what he knows is hidden within in the right time to appear and do its work. He is found studying the Old Testament. He accepts God's plans as to himself.

Again there is long silence. Jesus is about thirty years old, still living in the humble carpenter's home in Nazareth, when John the Baptist, a strenuous reformer, appears at the Jordan, drawing crowds and baptizing many in the acceptance of the rigorous life he enjoins. To him Jesus goes. John immediately recognizes him as superior to himself, introducing and commending to him his choicest disciples; and Jesus' public ministry begins.

As if himself somewhat startled by the sudden-
ness of his call, Jesus retires in solitude for some
forty days of self-scrutiny and inward struggle.
He emerges thoroughly prepared, and throws
himself into his work, winning an immediate following from men who are to be his permanent
disciples, and working miracles which startle the
beholders and widely spread his fame.

The subsequent story covers a period of only
three years. The first was one of comparative
obscurity. He limits his mission largely to Judea
and the immediate neighborhood of Jerusalem.
He seems to be watching the effect of his mission
upon the Jews at the center of influence, or to be
giving time for an effect he is seeking. After the
first, what attention he attracts is largely hostile;
and eventually he withdraws, driven out by fear
of Herod, as he had taken up successfully the
work of John the Baptist after Herod had cast
that troublesome reformer into prison.

The center of his ministry was now transferred
to Galilee. The second year was attended with
great success. Crowds everywhere flocked about
him. Miracle followed miracle, each more notable than the other. He healed the sick, gave sight
to the blind, made the lame to walk, restored the
leper, and even raised the dead. He does not definitely proclaim himself the expected Messiah of
Israel, and, indeed, does not say much about him-

self. He seems chiefly absorbed in doing good
and in teaching the kingdom of God as come in
him and illustrated in the life he leads. He gives
a great deal of time to a small group of men he
is training for the apostolate. His addresses are
remarkable, and his character comes out as peculiarly gracious, beautiful, and strong. He is always
calm and self-contained, impressing all with his
sinless perfection, and manifestly filled with an
absorbing love for men. He never is too weary
or too occupied to respond to any opportunity of
service to even the humblest.

The turning-point of his success occurs at the
opening of the third year. Returning from a brief
retirement with his disciples, a multitude met him
on the northeastern side of the Sea of Galilee.
Attracted at once by their need—for it was toward the close of a summer's day, and they were
tired, hungry, and far from their homes—he
wrought the notable miracle of feeding them
with the bits of barley-bread and the little fish
that constituted the uneaten lunch of a lad.

Awakening to what had been done, the multitude burst into loud applause, hailing him as the
Messiah, and proposing to march at once with
him to Jerusalem. Aware of the superficial and
unworthy character of their conceptions, he immediately withdrew; and when they saw that he
was unprepared or unwilling to accept their sup-

port, with the characteristic fickleness of a mob
the crowd fell away from him, many who were
beginning to call themselves his disciples turning
back.

He seems to have accepted the situation without perturbation or dismay. He begins quietly
to talk to the innermost circle of the disciples of
his failure and the certainty of his death. He
spends some six months with his disciples in retirement on the northern borders of Galilee, keeping out of the cities and even out of the public
thoroughfares. Then in an open and somewhat
formal manner he sets out for Jerusalem. Crowds
again gather about him; his fame spreads far
and wide; he says and does many wonderful
things; but though the people seem even more
ready than before to surrender themselves to him,
his own spirit is not expectant. When he reaches
the neighborhood of Jerusalem he retires again
into obscurity, emerging only to bring back to
life his friend Lazarus, who in his absence has
sickened and died.

As the Passover approaches and the crowds increase, he reappears. He ascends by the main
highway from Jericho to Jerusalem, attended by
a great gathering of people coming to the feast.
Rumor has spread that he is coming, and crowds
flock out of the city to meet him. Seized with a
sudden impulse, they begin to wave branches they

have broken from the trees ; and bursting into the Hallel—their national hymn of praise—they proclaim him king. Seated on an ass, quietly accepting the tributes of the people, he enters the city. Several days follow, in which he appears daily in the temple, discoursing much of his constant theme, the kingdom of God as at hand, and healing all who come to him, but making no attempt to profit by the support of the people, or even to create a party in his own favor.

At last the Jewish leaders, watching him closely, and noting his seeming carelessness, or his failure to profit by his opportunity, bribe one of his disciples to betray him. As he withdraws from the city in the evening, according to his custom, he is seized, hurried before a hastily called meeting of the sanhedrim, promptly tried and convicted, and then taken before the Roman governor Pilate for formal condemnation. There the charge is that he had refused tribute, that he had stirred up discontent, that he had made himself king, and finally, that he called himself the Son of God. To all this he made no reply further than quietly to demur to the manifest untruth of the preliminary accusations, and to admit and reaffirm the last.

You all know the story of Pilate's painful struggle. He seemed to be on trial rather than his prisoner, so certain was he of Jesus' innocence, and yet himself so unprepared to protect him or to meet the consequences of his release. But there is no escape. Pilate yields, and Jesus is hurried away to crucifixion. We need not go into the details of that scene, the one event in all history. The Saviour is put to an awful death, amid circumstances so impressive that even nature seemed to stand still. Darkness enwrapped the sky, and the earth quaked. His death is unquestioned, and Christianity was, to all appearances, ended.

In fact, Christianity, the religion of the Lord Jesus Christ, the one permanent life-giving force in the world, then begins. For on the morning of the third day Jesus rose from the dead. He showed himself alive by many infallible proofs and to many witnesses. He proclaimed his sacrificial work accomplished and his true ministry begun. Henceforth he is to live in the hearts and lives of his followers. His witness is not to be sought in miracles—for after a few utterances of those who have personally known him, his message is sufficiently accredited—but it is to be had in Christianity, the new life from God that is fast possessing the world. To that our appeal is to-day. Here is Christianity, not so much a force everywhere entering into human society, laying the only enduring foundations for law, for freedom, for growth, for all blessing, but everywhere coming to the individual, to comfort, to restore, to guide, to uplift, to make new men and women in Christ Jesus—the life from God, which to-day has brought God near to us all. It must be accounted for. The only explanation lies in the confession of the Roman centurion standing at the foot of the cross: "Truly this was the Son of God."

VI

HOW FAR IS THE BIBLE INSPIRED?

" The change that has made our idea of man and society so unlike the ancient is a change that begins with the notion of God and his law that came through Moses. This is a simple matter of historic fact and certainty. No code of antiquity possessed, in anything like the same degree, so exalted a notion of man, of the rights of man, of the dignity of man's labor, of his duties, of his moral worth and obligations, of his claim to reap and possess the harvest of profit or of plenty his own hands had sowed."

FAIRBAIRN, " Religion in History," p. 137.

" It is the same narrative, and yet one would be blind not to perceive that the signification has become altogether different. What formerly expressed naturalistic conceptions of a singular grossness here becomes the garb of moral truths of the most exalted and most purely spiritual nature.

" Between the Bible and the sacred books of Chaldea there is all the distance of one of the most tremendous revelations which have ever been effected in human beliefs. Herein consists the miracle. Others may seek to explain this by the simple natural progress of the conscience of humanity; for myself, I do not hesitate to find in it the effect of a supernatural intervention of divine Providence; and I bow before the Lord God who inspired the law and the prophets." FRANÇOIS LENORMANT.

" The rationalism of this day will give you good words as far as they go, but will empty them of their meaning. It will say, in *its* sense, that the prophets spake by the Holy Ghost (i.e., as all which is good and true is spoken by inspiration of the Spirit of God), and will ask of you in exchange to drop the words, or at least the meaning, of the Creed, that God the Holy Ghost 'spake by the prophets.' It will say to you that the prophets were 'elevated by a divine impulsion,' and grant you 'an intensified presentiment,' but only in the sense common to the higher conditions of humanity, even unaided by the Grace of God. It will acknowledge a fallible inspiration—fallible even as to matters of every-day morality—and will ask of you to surrender the belief in the infallible. It will descant on the love of God, if you will surrender your belief in his awful Holiness and Justice; it will speak with you of Heaven, if you, with it, will suppress the mention of Hell." PUSEY, " Daniel," pp. 452, 453.

VI

HOW FAR IS THE BIBLE INSPIRED?

NO question is of more living interest than the question of inspiration. No faith is older in the human heart than faith in inspiration. The song, "If ye will inquire, inquire ye," has been the voice which men have heard in their hearts from the beginning; and in spite of all the effects of transgression and all the allurements of the things that are seen conspiring to shut men out from the things that are not seen, the heart of man has insisted upon believing that that inclination to inquire of the unseen is genuine, and that it brings to him possibilities which are the noblest and the most needed of any of which he is conscious. In all forms of religion, in all ages of the world, men have believed that the gods have found some way to communicate their thoughts and desires to their worshipers, some way of opening to them definite knowledge of duty.

Now the question before us as Christians is not what there may be of inspiration in other religions, for Christianity differs from all other religions in that it presents a book as containing a record of all that God has vouchsafed to do in revealing himself and in opening a way of salvation for men ; and it holds that the book contains so full a record of that revelation that nothing need be added to it either for the guidance of the church or the salvation of the individual.

We do not ask whether some hymn that we love is inspired, such as " Jesus, lover of my soul," for example ; or some mighty poem that has spoken to the human heart for centuries ; or some moving piece of music ; or some ancient liturgy ; for we are persuaded, in common with the Christian world, that all there is of worth in the hymn or poem or song or liturgy came from the Word of God. No new spiritual truth has been given to the world outside of this book ; the sources and sanction of all are to be found here. Therefore for the Christian to-day the question of inspiration is as to what is the evidence that the writings within these covers differ from all other writings, and differ to this extent.

The church—as it believes, under the divine guidance—has been led to select these writings and preserve them in this form, and then to consider the collection a complete guide and rule for the Christian life ; so that the church now only asks for growing light to understand the Bible.

One thing ought to be said at the beginning, and that is, if any man is not a Christian the question of inspiration is not for him; for if these writings are the authentic record of God's dealings with men—that is, if they were written by men who were honest and trustworthy—then, wholly apart from their inspiration, they are sufficient to mark for every man the path of personal duty with reference to repentance and faith in the love of God. The church presents the book chiefly as the testimony of men who lived in the times of which they wrote, and who knew that that of which they wrote really took place; and it now offers it to every man as furnishing a sufficient guide in the way of life. The experience of men, in all lands and in all ages, has been that no matter what may be thought of the method in which these writings were produced, or whatever may be their relation to the unseen God, they are sufficient to lead any inquiring mind to the light and to the truth. So that faith in God, repentance for sin, and an opening path of peace are offered to all, wholly apart from any doctrine of inspiration. The question of inspiration is to be determined afterward—after the man has come to know for himself what there is in the Bible. Then it will be of interest to him to know more about this book which has done so much for him. How came it to be what it is?

In answering this question we are compelled to take the Bible as a whole. We must take it in the light of its own history—this book which for so many centuries has been wrapped up with the tenderest feelings and the noblest experiences of human hearts. In earliest days the Christians were a group of persecuted people who gathered about the book, to whom it spoke of their God, who gained strength for daily service, encouragement for heroic action, and a beautiful serenity of life—all of which resulted in making their faith and their conduct entirely different from that which the world produced. And through the subsequent centuries the same has been true. In any land in which the Bible is read exactly the same scenes are reproduced. Whether among the savages of the South Pacific, or in central Africa, or among the Indians on our far Western plains, or in any community in Europe, wherever a group gathers about the Bible it is found to be all that it has been from the beginning—a comfort, a strength, an inspiration, alike to the individual and the community. What glorious and precious memories cluster about it! It is the book of our childhood; the book that has been instrumental in regulating our own growing manhood; the book that everywhere is regarded as laying the foundation of all civilized society, and to-day means more to the world and is doing

more for the world than all other literature com-
bined.

Now, when we begin to ask questions about
the Bible, or, more particularly, to ask questions
of it, we find it full of God. Ask about nature.
It says that nature came from God: " In the beginning God created the heaven and the earth."
Ask about man. God made man " in his own
image." Ask about the unfolding of the life of the
Jews. " The Lord talked with Moses," " and God
spake all these words "—as he led his people out
of Egypt. So with the Psalms. They are full of
God. " O God, thou art my God," is the joyful
testimony. The prophets came bearing the burden of the law on their hearts. What they had
received, whether they understood the meaning
of the message or not, they delivered as a message from God. And when, in the New Testament, the Saviour begins to speak of the coming
of the kingdom of God, he represents it as fulfilled
in himself. This, then, is the first answer to the
question, Why has the Bible to-day this power
over human hearts? It is full of God. Wherever men open it, it always answers them with
something new about God; and that something
new about God has always been characteristic of
a revelation.

At the beginning the Bible tells us of God's
doings, of God's character, of God's purposes and

plans; and no man could have derived this knowledge in any other way than by what we call " revelation." It contains the record of God's dealings
with men.   It is true that God sometimes spoke
to men whose names we do not know; but we
have here an authentic record of a progressive
series of revelations leading to a definite result.

And as we read the record we find that it is
characterized by a singular vitality.   It is not such
truth as we read in the newspapers—a great deal
of which has no value to us.   The characteristic
of these truths is that they have been marked by
a singular productiveness, and wherever they have
been given to men the lives of men have begun at
once to change for the better.

Our Hebrew Bible, as you doubtless all know,
is divided into three parts.   The first is from
Adam to Moses.   The second embraces the
prophets and the Psalms, forming a progressive revelation from Moses to Malachi.   Then a
third group, made up of various miscellaneous
books—Chronicles, Ecclesiastes, Proverbs, Job,
etc.—gives what we may call the record of the
assimilation of this revelation.

The New Testament takes this in the first instance as sufficient authority, and bases its own
right to a hearing on what it finds of the prophecies that have proved true, adding what it has
received in the same fashion.   Jesus Christ stands

before his hearers and appeals to those things recorded in the Old Testament, in which " holy men
of God spake as they were moved by the Holy
Ghost." The Bible thus gives us first-hand knowledge about God and his relations to men, and then
it makes clear how God has been working in these
directions through all the centuries. Its purpose
is " not to show what the Jews were doing for God,
but rather what God was doing for the world
through the Jews."

Now there are two distinct sets of questions
about the Bible, just as there are two sets of questions about everything with which we have to deal
in life. I receive a telegram. I open it, and find
it is from a friend. It tells me where that friend
is, what he is doing, whether he is sick or well;
in short, all about him. Then I may ask, By what
line did the message come? how much were the
charges? who brought it? when did it arrive?
—all questions that you recognize as relatively
unimportant.

So in regard to the Bible; there are two distinct
groups of questions: questions of high importance, Who is it from? what is the message?
etc.; questions of lesser importance, By whose
hand did it come? in what form? and at what
time? You see at once that the latter are relatively secondary. We have reason to be sure
that God sent this message, and that he secured

the proper means for sending it. We are also sure that men of all conditions have found it the message which their hearts have most needed. So the questions which are of the highest class verify themselves.

Then we come to ask, How did God communicate this? We may reply that there are two distinct answers to the question of inspiration. One is that God accomplished his purpose by " absolute inspiration "—that is, God spoke directly to men, and made them write as he wished, as one would dictate to a type-writer. But I believe that the church never held that view; and there is no evidence of this method in the use to which the Bible has been put.

On the contrary, there is abundant evidence that God used men of widely different kinds: now a shepherd like Amos, and now a city-bred man like Isaiah ; now a singer like David, and now some unknown writer like the author of the Book of Chronicles ; now a king, and now some humble peasant ; now a learned man like Paul, and now a man like Matthew the publican. He chose all kinds of men, who were alike in one single respect : that they were men who were willing to be wholly men of God. " God at sundry times and in divers manners spake . . . unto the fathers by the prophets." The one universal characteristic of all the men through whom God has sent his message

to the world is that they were men who were willing to surrender themselves to be used by God's
Spirit, and that God used them just as they were,
and so they spoke with their whole being; as when
Jeremiah, for example, called to deliver his message to the people who were about to be led
away into captivity, feels himself but a child; and
Moses delivered his message with "stammering
speech." But in every instance, when the Spirit
of the Lord came upon them their whole personality went into the message. John has written
for us the message which no one could have
written but the beloved disciple—he who was
nearest to the Master, and leaned upon his
breast; Paul, one of the bravest of men, who
laid down his life, "counting it not dear unto
himself," has written another charged with all the
earnestness of his intense and consecrated nature.
The difference between the two messages is the
difference between the two men!

A friend sends to me a message of the recovery
of some dear one of whose life all had despaired.
He is anxious only that I shall receive the message quickly. What matters it if it comes on the
lips of a child or of a servant, provided I may trust
the messenger? And so God has sent to the
world this revelation of himself, giving a portion
of it to each of many different messengers.

Then, when we open to any one of these books

we find everywhere testimony to this fact—the consciousness of the inadequacy of the messenger himself. He feels himself "slow of speech," he finds himself "as a child," or he speaks of himself, as Paul did, as "in speech contemptible"; and in many instances the message is too large for the man. Paul spoke of having seen things which it was not lawful for him to utter, as did John in his apocalyptic vision. In each instance there is a divine guidance sufficient to make up for the inefficiency of the man. It is an adequate inspiration; God has a purpose, and he sees that it does not fail.

Now that is what we are to understand by inspiration. It is God's presence in the men through whom he spoke, securing the truth of the utterance in such a way that it shall be adequate to the divine purpose. The Bible may be faulty because of the human instrumentalities used, just as any message is faulty on human lips. It is unnecessary to prove it absolutely devoid of mistakes. It is historical, veracious, trustworthy. This we can prove. Furthermore, it speaks to our hearts. We hear it. We recognize it as the voice of our Father. Now the Bible could never have been what it is but for the Holy Spirit guiding men to write the truth which had at first been made known to their hearts. It is infallible, then, so far as is essential to lead men to God; for God's

Spirit guided it for that particular purpose. We have proof abundant that it is true in this respect. Beyond that we make no claim. God has spoken to men in this way so that they might hear his voice and know him; and, hearing his voice and knowing him, they find life in believing his words.

How far, then, is the Bible inspired? It is inspired so far as to make these writings an authoritative message from God to man. In this respect it differs from all other writings. Inspiration, if it is, as some claim, a present possession of the human heart, has now this as its sole function: not to give new messages, but to help men to interpret the message which God has given once for all through the men selected for that purpose. The messenger who is sent to me with a message from a sick friend was not sent to teach me how to spell or how to read English. He was sent to tell me all about that friend—his condition, his hope of recovery. So when God's messengers were sent to men they were sent for the single purpose of telling them about him. In the one case, as in the other, I must make out the message under the limitations of the messenger.

Nor is the Bible so far inspired as to compel us to seek evidence of the same manner of inspiration in all the writings. As I have shown you, God has spoken in different ways through these different men. " A little child shall lead them ;" and many a man who has been wandering from God finds his heart touched, and his conscience awakened, by the prattling questions of his little child—asking him why he is not a Christian, and why he does not pray ; and so the congregation which has not been stirred by any eloquence is melted to tears by the broken sentences of some ignorant man who rises to tell what God has done for his soul. God chooses the foolish things of this world to confound the wise, and the weak things to overcome the mighty. He uses ignorant men to bear his message because he will have us intent to hear, not man's voice, but God's.

VII

JESUS' DOCTRINE OF THE KINGDOM OF HEAVEN

" The unaccomplished mission of Christianity is to reconstruct society on the basis of brotherhood. What it has to do it does, and will do, in and through organization. At once profoundly individual and profoundly socialistic, its tendency to association is not so much an incident of its history as an essential element of its character. It spiritualizes that ineradicable instinct which draws man to man, and makes society not a convention, but a necessity." HATCH, " Bampton Lectures," p. 216.

VII

JESUS' DOCTRINE OF THE KINGDOM OF HEAVEN

THE sentiment running through all these hymns in which we have united with the Christian world to-day (Palm Sunday) in praising the Lord Jesus Christ as Lord and King is enough to show to any thoughtful mind that the conception of the kingdom as connected with Jesus Christ is something entirely different from the conception that goes with that word in its ordinary use. And that idea of the kingdom of Jesus Christ has just now gained a great hold upon the thoughts of men. It is not only widely discussed, but it is recognized as carrying within itself the panacea which is to furnish healing for the ills under which the world is suffering. This is not too much to expect of the kingdom of God.

It is important for us to understand what the kingdom of God is, and what are the methods by which it is to do its work, lest we be tempted to impatience with its ways, or mistake the signs of the times as to our own duty. The first words on the lips of the Saviour were regarding the gospel of the kingdom.   It was the message of glad tidings, and yet something more than a message.   It was already the gospel, in the sense in which we understand that word in the light of all the Christian centuries in which the Spirit of God has been dwelling in the hearts of men, making real to a multitude the personal experience of the new birth.   So that as the Saviour preached to a suffering world the gospel of the kingdom, he, at least, was conscious that he was proclaiming the new power and the new life for the world.

In this respect the gospel of the kingdom on the lips of the Saviour differed entirely from the kingdom of heaven which John the Baptist proclaimed as at hand.   The Saviour said of John that he was the greatest of the prophets, and yet he was only the herald of the new kingdom.   He was a Jew filled with the conception of the coming Messiah that then occupied men's minds, and yet so far inspired of God as to be free from many of the crudities and absurdities to which the Jews were subject.   Still the only gospel which John was permitted to utter was elementary.   He said to the assembled people, " Let each do right ; oppress no man ; be content with what you earn." As he saw multitudes hanging upon his words, only to turn away conscious that they had received a message too heavy for them, he settled into despondency, and there rested upon him that shadow of despair and isolation which already rested in a greater degree upon all the world. So that we think of John the Baptist as one dwelling apart, as " the voice of one crying in the wilderness," out of touch with the world, because he was conscious that the world did not receive his message.

How different are the first utterances of the Saviour, in which he proclaimed the kingdom of heaven as already come! The nature of the kingdom he announced was made plain at the very outset. You remember his interview with the Jewish rabbi at night, and how he summed up in a single sentence the whole condition of things: " Except a man be born again, he cannot enter [cannot even see] the kingdom of heaven." Here is one proclaiming a method new as compared with any that John the Baptist had taught; bringing to men, at the very beginning, hope, as well as the promise of pardon and a new life. And not only was this to begin with the power of God coming down into the hearts and lives of sinful and despairing men, but it was also to be, in all its relations, a spiritual kingdom; it was to work from within outward. " My kingdom is not of this world," was the Saviour's final answer to Pilate. " Neither shall they say, Lo here! or, lo there!" was another; " for, behold, the kingdom of God is within you."

This kingdom was already begun in the coming of Jesus himself into the world. It issued from his heart, and was seen in his beautiful life. It passed out from him in his deeds; as when he took by the hand the dead daughter of Jairus, and said unto her, " Maid, arise. And her spirit came again, and she arose straightway." The method of that divine life—working outward from within—the Saviour did not explain. He simply illustrated it. It was left to the writers of the Epistles to explain it more fully; Paul sums it all up when he says, " What the law could not do, in that it was weak through the flesh, God sending his own Son in the likeness of sinful flesh, and for sin, condemned sin in the flesh." " What the law could not do "—that is, John the Baptist and the prophets; because no effort on the part of man could forgive sin—what the law could not do even in its best estate, God sending his own Son in the likeness of sinful flesh has done : a new life has entered the heart of every man who believes. The kingdom of heaven has come, and is within you.

Now what is the result of the Spirit of God coming into the hearts of men ? " He that raised up Christ from the dead shall also quicken your mortal bodies," says Paul. Now we understand why it is that we are called to be perfect even as Jesus is perfect; why all are to put on the likeness of

Jesus Christ. We are all in the church as one body, all helping one another. We are to attain at last to the measure of the stature of the perfect man, which is to be like Christ. It is only the fulfilment, the accomplishment, of the divine Spirit working in us. You see it in the life of every man who has accepted Christ. Go to any mission in this city and listen to the story of one of the saved men. He will say: " I was a drunkard, a prodigal, a gambler; and so many months, weeks, or nights ago I came into this mission, and here I heard the story of Jesus Christ's dying to save poor, weak, fallen men. I felt myself the lowest of the low, the vilest of the vile; and I got down on my knees and said, ' O God, canst thou save such a man as I am? I believe thou art not only able, but willing.' And God heard my prayer; a new life came into my heart, and a new song in my mouth, even praises to his name. I went out of this place with the same old clothes on, the same man externally; but within all was changed. I knew I had a new heart. Old things had passed away; behold, all things had become new. Ever since that time I have loved the things that God loves, and hated the things that God hates. I have turned away from drink and gambling and bad companions, and in the place of misery and unrest I have a loving wife and a happy home; in short, the garden of my life has begun to blossom in the Lord Jesus Christ."

That story can be heard every day and night in New York, or wherever a company of Christians gather to tell what the Lord has done for their souls. But that is not all; for the Apostle proceeds, in that eighth chapter of Romans, to tell how "the whole creation groaneth and travaileth in pain together until now." He describes the condition of the world as it is to-day. But he goes on to say it is waiting for the redemption which God in his own good time is going to accomplish even for nature. That, then, is the fulfilment of the coming of the kingdom of God, of which Christ proclaimed merely the outward fact; and this is the method of it: it begins by making a man new in his own eyes because he is new in God's eyes; and the light works from him outward until nature itself is blessed. The darkness falls from the eyes of the blind; the tongue of the dumb is loosed; the ears of the deaf are unstopped; and to the poor the gospel is preached, without money and without price. The law of the kingdom is simply the law of love. "The Son of man came not to be ministered unto, but to minister, and to give his life a ransom for many." This, then, is the law of the kingdom: "Love the Lord thy God with all thy heart, and with all thy soul, and with all thy strength, and with all thy mind," in order that the new life may be realized in you; and then "love thy neighbor as thyself."

Here we have also the conditions of the growth of the kingdom. How many illustrations there were of the power of his love in the brief years of the Saviour's ministry! How it at once changed the lives of those with whom he came in contact! He is talking with the woman at the well—a woman so degraded and hopeless that she was despised by her companions and reduced to the necessity of toiling drearily for a living. But how that heart and mind enlarged under the truth which Jesus revealed to her! "If thou knewest the gift of God, and who it is that saith to thee, Give me to drink; thou wouldest have asked of him, and he would have given thee living water. Whosoever drinketh of this water shall thirst again: but whosoever drinketh of the water that I shall give him shall never thirst; but the water that I shall give him shall be in him a well of water springing up into everlasting life." How her ears opened to that declaration! "God is a Spirit: and they that worship him must worship him in spirit and in truth." What a revelation to her soul! Now she is hungering and thirsting for a knowledge of the new life that comes from God. A new impulse has come into her heart. At once she forgets herself; she leaves her water-pot, she runs back to the city, and going

into the very circle where her life was a shame
and a reproach, she cries out, " Come, see a man,
which told me all things that ever I did: is not
this the Christ?" "And many of the Samari-
tans of that city believed on him for the saying
of the woman, which testified, He told me all
that ever I did." "And many more believed
because of his own word"—because they had
heard him for themselves. See how quickly the
work was done; it was like the sudden opening
of a flower.

So it was, again, with the Syrophenician woman.
She had a sick child, and she besought Jesus that
he would heal her. Jesus replied, " It is not meet
to take the children's bread, and to cast it unto the
dogs." "And she answered and said unto him,
Yes, Lord: yet the dogs under the table eat of
the children's crumbs." How quick the wit!
how keen the insight! And Jesus, looking with
amazement upon her said, " For this saying go
thy way; the devil is gone out of thy daughter."
The transformation had begun in a moment, just
as the life begins in a man, or in a church or a mission, or anywhere, when ears are opened. First
of all, believe in the divine life that is in Jesus,
and then recognize that that life attests itself by
working from within outward. The summons is
to our whole being, and the response is in new
powers. The believer grasps larger thoughts,

feels a larger life, and is indeed a new man in Christ Jesus.

Now what are some of the agencies by which the kingdom is doing its work in the world? First there is the family. The husband and wife become conscious of a new power in their own hearts, with their first knowledge of their love for each other. The love of the husband and the wife, God-given, centers in the life of their child; and, as that life unfolds, the family is set up, becoming the true unit of the kingdom. In it permanent, progressive life becomes possible. Then there is the state, a combination of families for the common good, in which the administration is of all and by all and for the best good of all. Then there is the necessity of daily toil, as the great gift of God to man, and all forms of trade and commerce in which man's well-being is promoted. Art and literature are its servants, and science of every kind, as they carry its message or open the way for its progress. Then there are all the schemes of moral reform for the elevation of politics, for improving the condition of the poor, for the prevention of cruelty, and the like. All these become at once testimony to the establishment of the kingdom among men, and the mighty instruments by which God is doing his work in the world.

Then we come to the church, as practically

identical with the progress of the kingdom. You remember how it was announced by the Lord at Cæsarea Philippi. The shadow of the cross had begun to reach out toward the Saviour as he talks to his followers about his death. He asked, "Whom do men say that I, the Son of man, am?" And they replied in one way and another. "But whom say ye that I am?" Peter exclaimed, "Thou art the Christ, the Son of the living God." Jesus replied, "Blessed art thou, Simon Bar-jona: for flesh and blood hath not revealed it unto thee, but my Father which is in heaven. And I say also unto thee, that thou art Peter, and upon this rock I will build my church; and the gates of hell shall not prevail against it." So the church becomes at once identical with the kingdom. The kingdom, as we have seen, begins with the coming of the Spirit of God into a man's heart; and the Saviour says that is where the church begins. Before the man makes his confession the kingdom is unobservable. It may be real. The man has the gift of life, but he is not aware of it. The moment he stands by Peter's side and makes Peter's confession, that moment he takes his place in the kingdom.

Now you see what the characteristics of the new kingdom are. It is founded on Jesus, just as it had its beginning in him. It is testified to by his followers. In the church it finds its home. The much-mooted question to-day is, Is the church really the kingdom of God? Will not the kingdom be brought about more effectually if men turn from the church and go out into the world to busy themselves with its reforms and philanthropies—setting aside the question of religion and taking up simply that of morality? Now the fact is that those times in which morality has been most talked about are the times when it has been practised the least. In the last century Bishop Butler said he visited many different churches in London, and could not tell from anything he heard whether the preacher believed in Christ, Buddha, or Mohammed. The church was preaching the kingdom of God then as society would have us preach it to-day. But how did Christ answer the world which was seeking to find the kingdom of God outside the church? The answer came in the revival under the Wesleys and Whitefield, in which the world was called back to the central truth that there is no kingdom except where it is found in the individual heart, and where Christ is made its center and end. The answer to the worldly kingdom of the eighteenth century is the Spirit-filled kingdom of the nineteenth century—the most wonderful century in all the Christian history; the century of foreign missions, the Sunday-school, the Young Men's Christian Association, great and wide-reaching philanthropies and educational movements, and, above all, of that true form of Christian socialism which is calling upon the rich and the wise to come out of their palaces and their sanctums and make their wealth and their knowledge contribute to the good of their fellow-men. Men point to the Salvation Army as an indication of what may be done outside of the church. Where did it arise? From what does it draw much of its power to-day? From men in the church. It is only one of the many forms of the church. It is made up of men who are giving to Christ his proper place in their lives, and, in open confession of him, working ever in the blessed consciousness of the indwelling power of the Holy Ghost.

What, then, are the promises of the permanency of the kingdom of God for the future? Jesus said, " Lo, I am with you alway, even unto the end of the world;" " It is expedient for you that I go away: for if I go not away, the Comforter will not come unto you; but if I depart, I will send him unto you." Because the Spirit of God abides in the church we have the promise and guaranty that the church of God will abide; that it will remain true to its Master, and that the trust that has been committed to it will be kept unto the end.

The Saviour illustrated this in many beautiful ways. Take the parable of the sower. Some of the seed falls into good soil, some among thorns, some on the rocks where there is little depth of earth. All grow together until the harvest. You remember the parable well. So it is with the church. How often men have said to me, " I never could become a member of your church while such and such a man is in it ; I never could sit in church with such a man "! The tares and the wheat grow up together. " Let every one that nameth the name of Christ depart from iniquity," is the law ; we must continue in the world in order to meet the test.

Take the parable of the wedding-feast. Those that were bidden would not come, and the king said to his servants, " The wedding is ready, but they which were bidden were not worthy. Go ye therefore into the highways, and as many as ye shall find, bid to the marriage ;" and so the wedding was crowded with guests—just as to-day you see Japan, China, and the far islands of the sea coming into the kingdom, and many right here in New York still without.

But the final time for the kingdom is illustrated by the parable of the mustard-seed. Christ said it was " like to a grain of mustard-seed, which a man took, and sowed in his field : which indeed is the least of all seeds : but when it is grown, it is the greatest among herbs, and becometh a tree, so that the birds of the air come and lodge in the branches thereof." These are all proofs of the permanency of the kingdom. It is of the Lord, purchased by his precious blood, watched over by his unceasing love. And the triumph of the kingdom is at hand; "but of that day and hour knoweth no man, no, not the angels of heaven, but my Father only."

Now what are the conditions of membership in the kingdom? "Jesus called a little child unto him, and set him in the midst of them, and said, Verily I say unto you, Except ye be converted, and become as little children, ye shall not enter into the kingdom of heaven." The kingdom goes on its benign way, doing its blessed work among men; and will you continue to stand by the wayside sneering at it? You understand nothing of it, and never will, until you come as a little child, freed from self-righteousness and false pride; come to receive and not to give; saying, "Lord, what wilt thou have me to do? Give me a place in thy kingdom." Until men come in that way they can have no part or lot in it. Nor can they do anything that will really count in the work of the world until they have found the life of the kingdom in their own hearts. Without that they are walking and working in darkness. Without that they are building a house on the sands; and the wind and storm will come and beat upon it, and it will fall.

VIII

WHY DOES NOT GOD CONVERT MEN?

" If it is necessary, viewed from any standpoint, that eventually men *must* be reconciled to God, then human freedom is only seeming."   ULRICI, " Gott und die Natur," p. 727.

" I am a nobler substance than the stars; or are they better since they are bigger ?   I have a will and faculties of choice—to do or not to do, and reason why I do or not do this—the stars have none.   They know not why they shine, more than this taper; nor how they work, nor what."   OLD DRAMA.

VIII

WHY DOES NOT GOD CONVERT MEN?

THERE are those who stumble before this question: " If God is all-powerful and all lives are in his hand, and if he is a loving God, why does he not make men what he wants them to be?" The question is connected with many of the most intricate problems of human life—the problem of sin, and why it exists; the problem of pain, and its meaning; and of future punishment. No one can live long in this world without sooner or later being crowded up against these mysteries. After the great German preacher and philosopher, Schleiermacher, had lost his only son he said: " Many have written me letters which they intended to be words of comfort. They said to me, ' God has taken away your child, perhaps to save him from the evils of the world;' and my heart at once replied, ' Could not God who gave him to me keep him from those evils and still leave him with me?' Others have written, ' God has taken away your child because he would chasten you;'

and my heart answered, 'Must God cut off the beautiful life of my boy in order to chasten me, his father?' No, there is no comfort for me in such suggestions." Where did he find his consolation? He said: "Only when I let myself sink as a little child into the arms of my Father, content to rest in those arms, knowing nothing more than that they are about me, am I sustained and comforted."

And yet those questions do arise, and always have arisen, and must be dealt with. An incident in the Saviour's life shows how pertinent they were in his day. John tells us, in the tenth chapter of his Gospel, that as Jesus was walking in the temple, in Solomon's porch, certain of the Jews came to him. It was after he had been doing many of his most notable miracles, and when everything about him suggested the revelation which God was making. They said, "How long dost thou make us to doubt? If thou be the Christ, tell us plainly." It was a natural desire. Men want conclusive evidence. They want to know what God does and why he does it. On every side there are those who are in earnest; why, then, does not God do what he wants to have done? Why does he not disclose that concerning himself and his ways which, perhaps, would lead men into light and peace? This is the question before us.

In this case what had the Saviour already re-

vealed of himself? It was the winter before the
crucifixion, so that his whole ministry lay behind
him. What that ministry was you all know.
At the very beginning he had laid claim to being
the Messiah, and had been recognized as such.
John himself tells us of the interview with Nathanael, in which Jesus, seeing Nathanael coming
unto him, said of him, " Behold an Israelite indeed, in whom is no guile!" Nathanael answered, " Whence knowest thou me?" Jesus replied, " Before that Philip called thee, when thou
wast under the fig-tree, I saw thee;" and Nathanael answered him, " Rabbi, thou art the Son
of God; thou art the King of Israel." Then had
come those later interviews with Nicodemus
and others, in which he opened the deepest
truths to men's hearts, and professed such divine
knowledge that there could be no question as to
what he, at least, held himself to be. He said,
for example, in the fifth chapter of John : " Verily,
verily, I say unto you, The Son can do nothing
of himself, but what he seeth the Father do : for
what things soever he doeth, these also doeth the
Son likewise"—claiming oneness in power, in
scope of work, with the Father himself. And
again in the same chapter he uttered the most
conclusive claim : " For as the Father hath life in
himself; so hath he given to the Son to have life
in himself."

At the very beginning he had asserted his oneness with the Father, and had said that he was the center and source of that light and life which, coming from God, had reached the heart of man; and to sustain that affirmation he had wrought the miracles, the effect of which was to lead men to believe. All his discourses had pointed out the facts concerning himself and his mission. Yet here were men who had seen all and heard all, but who found themselves separated from others, in that others believed while they did not. They come and say to him, " If you want us to believe, why do you not give us evidence which will compel us to believe? " Just as men say to-day, " If God wants us to be Christians, why does he not make us Christians? "

This at once raises some important questions. How is belief accomplished? What brings about conversion in any life? On all sides men say, " Give us facts! "—as if the mere presentation of facts brings conviction. But surely something more than this is necessary.

Take an illustration. How, for example, do you see? In the field of vision there are always innumerable objects—hundreds of faces before me now; in the street, hundreds of signs over the shops and stores as you pass. You do not see them all, although they are all before your eyes, until suddenly your attention is arrested; then you observe that sign or notice that person. Something more is necessary than the mere presence of an object.

The same thing is true of the ear. How do you hear? I was talking, not long ago, with an engineer in his engine-room, when suddenly he sprang forward and turned a handle. I asked him why he did that, and he looked at me in surprise. "Did you not hear the click of that valve?" "No," I said, "I did not." Now, wherein lay the difference between us—my hearing, probably, being as acute as his? The difference was in the fact that his ear was governed by something that lay back in his purpose. The possession of what we call "attention" enabled him to hear what I did not hear, producing effects and movements in him which were not produced in me.

Thus we realize that something more is needed than the mere presentation of the object. An object is seen or not seen, heard or not heard, produces an effect or fails to produce it, according to the existence of something that lies wholly within ourselves. There was a striking illustration of this fact in Professor Pasteur's discovery of important dissimilarity in the crystals of two salts. When the announcement was made, Professor Mitscherlich, his colleague, said that he had himself so carefully observed those crystals without discovering any difference that Pasteur could never have noticed it except his observation had been "guided by some preconceived idea," something within himself, some purpose, some governing thought in his own mind, wholly independent of the external facts, the effect of which enabled him to see what lay before the eyes of others—equally well trained, equally in earnest—but which they could not see. Pasteur elsewhere himself speaks of these predetermined conceptions as "the vivifying flame of the sciences of observation."

This, then, may be accepted as the fundamental fact in the mind of man: observing a fact, appreciating the significance of a truth, depends upon something in ourselves. As Pascal said, long ago, " All truth is extant, only we fail to perceive it." All the facts concerning the universe, concerning the Lord Jesus Christ and his work, are more or less apparent, only some fail to regard them.

Now what had the Saviour to say concerning such men? And in answering this we answer the question, Why does not God do something more than present to us the truth? Jesus answered them : " I told you, and ye believed not : the works that I do in my Father's name, they bear witness of me. But ye believe not, because ye are not of my sheep, as I said unto you. My sheep hear my voice, and I know them, and they

follow me : and I give unto them eternal life ; and
they shall never perish, neither shall any man
pluck them out of my hand." In other words,
he says that the reason why some hear and others
do not is because of that something in themselves,
something in their own will, which determines
their attitude toward him. Some have what may
be called an attention, a predetermined thought or
purpose, with reference to him, while others have
not.

And, furthermore, he says that the effect upon
those who will not hear is that they finally lose the
power of hearing. We long fail to observe, and
in time we lose the power of observation. We
long fail to regard the truth concerning God and
Jesus Christ, and in time that truth vanishes from
our conception, as John records, in the prophet's
words, in regard to the Jews. He says that
" Esaias said again, He hath blinded their eyes,
and hardened their heart ; that they should not see
with their eyes, nor understand with their heart,
and be converted, and I should heal them." Or
as in the parable of the sower, where the evil one
comes and snatches away the seed, though some
of it is in good soil, where, if it were allowed to
remain, it would spring up and bear fruit.

Then the Saviour adds, " No man can come
to me, except the Father which hath sent me
draw him." In other words, all the world would

reject him to-day, just as the Jews rejected him,
were it not for the fact that the Father moves
men's hearts, creating attention, desire, a preconceived determination which enables them to hear
what other men do not catch, to obtain what other
men lose. " Except the Father which hath sent
me draw " them, they will not come. Then the
promise he adds is, " If any man will do his will "
—or " wills to do his will "—" he shall know of
the doctrine, whether it be of God, or whether I
speak of myself." " The truth shall make him
free." If any man finds in his heart an earnest
purpose to know the truth he shall not be left to
grope without it.

Then we come to the question, What are the
characteristics of the Christian? What does
God require of you and me with regard to our
acceptance of the truth? Simply two things.
Men stumble over the question of religion, and
it is as plain as the day. God requires only two
things.

The first of these is that we will to know the
truth. This we can do. A child is studying.
He does not understand a problem in arithmetic.
His attention is elsewhere, his eyes are out of the
window intent upon watching something in the
street. The teacher makes it an object to the
child to understand the lesson, and at once it becomes plain. All that God asks of any man is

that he shall give attention to the truth; shall will
to know it, or, as we should say, be willing to receive it. In other words, he is to give the truth
which is already revealed his attention.

Now what is it that God has put within the
reach of inquiring minds to-day by which those
who are willing, who have a desire, who will give
their attention, can be won to the Christian faith?
There are three things which sum it all up.
What are they?

First, the Bible. It contains the story of what
God has been doing through all the centuries.
The Old Testament is not a history of what the
Jews did, it is a history of what God did for the
world through the Jews; the New Testament is
not a history of what the church or the apostles
did, but it is a history of what God accomplished
through the church and the apostles. Now we
know how Jesus came into the world; and we have
the story of his life; and we know how, beginning
with the apostles, the early church was led—its
records are extant. A gentleman said to me the
other day, "The fact is, a great many men do not
believe in Christianity because they have an impression that the history of Christianity is very
incomplete, and they had better not make any inquiries about it back of the sixth century. Before
that time it is all a mystery." I said in reply,
"There is no reason why any man should have

such a view." " No," he replied, " I suppose not ; but somehow men have got the impression that there is not much to be known of early Christianity." Now those earlier centuries are fairly loaded down with facts concerning the life and progress of the Christian church. We know with what striking power of assimilation it took out of the world, on the right hand and on the left, thoughts and institutions and offices and methods to which it could impart its own spirit, and which it, in turn, could set at work in the various communities to which the gospel had come. We have a very substantial record of the church of God through the first Christian centuries until the world surrendered itself to the power of the church—a history that is in its main features as plain and as certain and as well attested as the history of the English constitution, or of the Anglo-Saxon race on our own continent.

Now God presents to every man to-day the Bible, with its testimony of facts concerning Jesus of Nazareth, his disciples, and those who followed them. Then, in addition, God presents to every man who will receive it Christianity as it is in the world—the organized power of the Christian life ; not scattered believers, but the organization which has withstood all the changes in civilization, all the great movements of nations from continent to continent, and has proved itself competent to uplift every group of men on the surface of the earth. It goes alike into the slums and into palaces, into the heart of Europe or America or Africa, and everywhere produces the same results, lifting men out of selfishness and drunkenness and idolatry and darkness, into the truth and the light; but always in proportion as men receive it in whole or in part. Those who accept the truth in its entirety, and surrender themselves, and their fears and their hopes and their business and their thoughts, to the Lord Jesus Christ, are always seen manifesting the same characteristics. They become pure and gentle and honest and truthful and unselfish, and have a faith that reaches to that within the veil. They become the leaven in the lump of society.

One other kind of evidence is presented: that is the voice in the heart. Men may try to satisfy themselves in the world, but they are not at rest. You business men try to be content with what you have gained—with your power or the riches you have piled up; but none of these things satisfy you. There are possessions richer, more enduring, more satisfying than any you have yet found. You are seeking honor in life: no matter what a good reputation you may have won, no matter how well you may have seemed to succeed, there is an unrest that is never dormant, never satisfied, until you come to know God and gain the hope of heaven. That is the unrest which compels men to ask, "What must I do to be saved?" What is this feeling in the soul but the testimony which God gives to every man concerning himself? And the one thing that God requires of every man is that he shall be willing to receive the testimony; that he shall give attention to it; that he shall have an earnest desire, amounting, if you will, to a predetermined purpose, to know the truth. "If there is a God, I would know him. If there is a Saviour for sinners, I would be found by him. If there is pardon for such a sinner as I am, I would receive that pardon. I would come as the publican did, saying, 'God be merciful to me a sinner.'" Now what God requires of every man first of all is that.

Then there is the other thing, namely, obedience to what follows the testimony. In the incident before us the Saviour said, "Ye believe not, because ye are not of my sheep, as I said unto you." "My sheep" are distinguished from you, and from all the world, by this one thing: that they "hear my voice and follow me." So that in order to be a Christian we must have a desire to be a Christian; and when we have a desire to be a Christian, then the testimony which God gives carries conviction; and when we find ourselves moved by the testimony, and we recognize that God is our Father, and that the Lord Jesus

Christ has died to save us, and that the voice in our hearts is calling upon us to love God and keep his commandments, then it is that we cry, "Lord, here am I: what wilt thou have me to do?"

Now I think we know why God will not convert men—because he cannot. He wants love, and we control our own affections. He wants obedience, and every man is master of his own will. Obedience is the spontaneous offering of a converted soul. And so, dear friends, all that God can do he has done for us. He has furnished all these heaped-up centuries of Christian testimony. He has kept alive in us this feeling of unrest, instead of allowing us to become stony-hearted and rebellious against the truth. He pleads with us every day, for our own sake, that we be his. He troubles us in all our daily life, because he cannot rest content until we become content to be his; and finally he brings us to that hour in which we must settle the question one way or the other—whether we will love, trust, and obey him, or not. And when we are willing to believe we find that his arms are thrown about us, and that his love is already filling our hearts.

I remember a scene which happened some years ago. A stranger knocked at the door of my study, and I bade him come in. He was a man in middle life, and evidently in great distress. I invited him to be seated, and he told me the story of his life. He was an actor, and was then connected with a traveling troupe. But for some weeks he had been so troubled on account of his sins that he could not rest. He finally decided to leave his company; and this he did one night when they were playing in a distant town. He came to me to have me tell him what to do to be saved. I tried to find out how it was that these thoughts came to him, and why he finally reached the decision he did. He could not tell. He had not been to church, nor in any way in contact with Christian people. He came to me simply because he knew that I was a minister, in the hope that I could show him what he should do. His repentance was sincere, his emotions were genuine, his desire to lead a better life was very earnest, but for some time I could give him no light. At last I put this question to him: " If you did not call these thoughts into your own mind, who did?" He thought for a few moments, and said, " God must have done it." " Very well," I said; " if God cared enough for you to follow you, to crowd the truth upon you at every turn, and to keep you in constant unrest until you felt that you could not live that life any longer, do you not think that he cares enough for you to forgive you and make you his child, if you will but give yourself to him now?" He looked at me for a moment, and then answered, "Yes, I do. If God cared enough for me not to let me lose this desire to lead a better life; if he cared enough for me to follow and keep me all these days and years in which I have wandered from him, I know I can trust him now when I want to be forgiven, and when I want to be a different man." With the tears running down his face he kneeled by my side and asked God to be merciful to him a sinner; and I am sure he went out of that room a forgiven and converted soul. He was ready to obey. Whatever God would have him do he longed to do. Can any man doubt that he was a Christian?

Now, dear friends, apply these truths to yourselves. All the testimony concerning God is extant; you need only to receive it. All the covenants of God for the Christian life are plain and open before you; you need only to obey. Begin now to follow Christ, and immediately Christ is yours and you are his. "My sheep" prove that they are mine in that they "hear my voice and follow me."

ל

IX

THE MANLINESS OF BEING PERSUADED

" There is one thing more deplorable than believing in error; that is, believing in nothing." DE PRESSENSÉ.

" I feel more and more the need of intercourse with men who take life in earnest. It is painful for me to be always on the surface of things. Not that I wish for much of what is called religious conversation ; that is often apt to be on the surface. But I want a sign which one catches by a sort of freemasonry that a man knows what he is about in life. When I find this it opens my heart with a fresh sympathy as when I was twenty years younger." DR. THOMAS ARNOLD.

IX

THE MANLINESS OF BEING PERSUADED

THE question of the last address, If God wants men to be better, why does he not make them so? is the negative side of the truth, the positive side of which I now desire to present. I want to show to you how the invitation, "Come unto me, all ye that labor and are heavy-laden, and I will give you rest," is the crowning glory of the religion of Jesus Christ.

In one of the supreme moments of the Apostle Paul's life he said, in that wonderful eighth chapter of Romans: "I am persuaded, that neither death, nor life, nor angels, nor principalities, nor powers, nor things present, nor things to come, nor height, nor depth, nor any other creature, shall be able to separate us from the love of God, which is in Christ Jesus our Lord." How much stronger, how much more satisfying that utterance is than if he had said, "I am compelled to take this position," or "I have been enticed into it"! "I am persuaded"—not even commanded.

An appeal has been made to me, an appeal to my
entire nature, and I have discovered that within
me which has responded to it, and now I plant
myself deliberately. I am ready to stake all that
I am, all that I have, and all that I hope to be,
upon the joint act of God and myself.

Notice the dignity of this method—God's
method of saving men by persuasion. It is,
you see at once, a method worthy of the parties
concerned. It is the act of Omnipotence and
Omniscience laying aside almighty power, taking
no advantage of the unique position of the eternal God, and dealing with man upon the plane of
man's need and man's nature, and leading him
thus gradually, as by the united act of two lovers
—a Father and a son—out into all the good that
is possible.

See what respect it shows to man as well as to
the Maker of man. God has made man in his own
image; and this is recognition, not of the " divinity
that shapes our ends," but of the divinity that is
in us, that can join with the Creator and be a
worker together with God. And it is a dignity
that grows out of the nature of the subject. God
has the power. God can create things even as
we see them in the world about us. He can do
what he will even with the manhood that he has
formed. But back of his creative power, at the
very center of the divine Being itself, lies the

truth; and this is the method of conviction—
through the truth. "I am the way, the truth,
and the life," said the Saviour. "Every one that
is of the truth heareth my voice." The method
by which God would save men, then, is digni-
fied. It not only reveals the glory of God, it
not only appeals to the manliness of men, but it
exalts that which in our thought we like to think
of as lying even back of God, as being the very
foundation itself of the divine character, namely,
the truth. God puts this forward in appealing
to men, and in so doing he lays the broad foundation upon which man's life and man's character and man's immortality and man's communion with God for eternity are henceforth to
rest.

Then see the sweet graciousness of this method.
The Almighty God, whose law has been broken,
whose power in his own realm has been defied,
lays aside the swift judgment which he might have
inflicted upon the sinner, and tries to win him back
to a life from which, in his wilfulness and rebellion,
if you will, he has departed; thus using the graciousness and winsomeness of the Saviour's life to
bring man not only into a condition of obedience,
but into a condition where the hardness shall melt
from his heart, the rebelliousness from his spirit,
and where gentleness and gratitude shall spring
up in every part of his being.

In the ordinary relations of life how grateful we are for the example and influence of some great man who has won us to higher ideals and renewed efforts in the battle of life! But the other day Professor Tyndall, the great scientist, died, and I was reminded in his death that one more of that group—young men who, thirty or forty years ago, made English science so distinguished—has passed away. It brought to my mind the beautiful biography of that other member of the same splendid group, Clerk Maxwell, who died all too early; and I remember the story he tells of the vision that opened to his dawning intellect of the possibilities of scientific discovery, and how it was the kindness of the great and beloved Professor Faraday that inspired him to larger achievement: by the humility he showed, and the respect he paid to the powers of the younger man, he supplied to him courage and hope, opening to his thought truths and possibilities which otherwise would have been closed.

Now, think of it: not a mere man, but the Lord of all, dealing with us by the method of persuasion! He wooing us to inquire of him concerning the truth; encouraging us to seek from him pardon; strengthening us by his grace in overcoming temptation; winning us to believe that there are possibilities in the prodigal far from his home, in the profligate lost in a great city, even in the woman that is an outcast, which are worth looking up and cultivating. Think of the great God coming down graciously to the sinner and, in the person of the Lord Jesus Christ, seeking to save that which was lost! Is there any possible relation of the divine Father comparable to this? Is there elsewhere such a conception of God—so loving the world as to give his only begotten Son to die for us, that we may be persuaded to repent?

See, also, the broad freedom of this method. In all the ordinary relations of life the conditions upon which a man is led out of his narrow life into the larger privilege of some other man's service are that he will surrender his freedom. He becomes the servant of some master who can give him large wages; he becomes the imitator, careful and exact, of some one who can open to him larger knowledge than he possesses.

Now, how different is God's method as he summons us, and summons the world, to the new life in Jesus Christ! We look back to the day when the Saviour came preaching the new gospel to the world, and how entirely different his method is from what we might have expected! The world was sunk in despair, until despair had settled upon the philosopher in his school, upon the statesman in the senate-chamber, upon the general in command of his army, upon the emperor on his throne.

Now suppose the gospel had come with sharp lashes; suppose it had sought to amend society immediately from the outside—its social life, its laws, its customs, its institutions, its forms of government; suppose it had instantly denounced slavery and polygamy—how narrow the method would have seemed! " Times change," the world would have said. " These are only passing incidents of the world's progress. Valuable as these reforms may be, they will be as transient as that which they amend. The world itself would have got rid of these forms of vice when they had become unendurable." "And how impossible it is!" the world would have said; " for while you mend the practices of a man you do not mend the man." We are perfectly familiar with this sort of dealing to-day. I remember some years ago hearing of a gentleman who arose to address a gathering made up largely of newsboys. Suddenly the thought came to him that he would seize the opportunity to rebuke them for using tobacco. Instantly every boy was spitting on the floor; and finally there was such an uproar and tumult that he had to stop. They would not listen to him at all.

Now, what has been the method of Christianity? We find nothing in the teaching of the Saviour or the apostles attacking society in its external forms; no indignation because the Jews at that time were under the dominion of Rome;

nothing said about the evils of the wine-shop, or the dangers of worldly amusements, or any of the social habits by which the world has ever been enthralled; but, on the contrary, there was a uniform effort to get into man's heart a new conception of righteousness, of redemption, and of love; a uniform effort to change the thoughts of man, that through his thoughts his heart and mind might be changed; always the attempt to plant seed in the soul which, by its own inherent force, as it grew, would change the outward life.

See how this method works to-day. The world is permeated with Christianity. It is found everywhere, supplying all that is most vital and valuable in human life. The historians have hastened to record that it was the renewing force of the gospel of Christ that changed Roman society, that stopped the gladiatorial shows, that transformed the Europe of the barbarous Goth into the Europe of to-day. It was the leaven hidden in the meal that worked through it; and the same method is the method of blessing everywhere to-day. A whole hour might be spent in illustrating this point.

In the suburbs of a Western city there lived a German family, consisting of a father, mother, and two children. The father kept a saloon, and the children attended a small mission Sunday-school not far distant. The blessing of God fell upon the school, and many of the scholars took Christ for their Saviour. Among others were the children of this saloon-keeper. The old story repeated itself: not content with their own peace and joy, they sought to win others. They went home and told their father and mother what had happened to them. Not long after the mother was seen in the evening meetings, and a little later the father. One evening, when an opportunity was given to Christians to tell what the Lord had done for them, the German saloon-keeper arose and said, " I sell no more vhisky." That was all —" I sell no more vhisky." The next morning the saloon was closed forever. There was no excitement, no band of praying women going in to take the place by storm ; but the grace of Christ manifested in that little mission-school, through the hearts of those little girls, had not only closed the saloon, but had closed the heart of the man to sin and opened it to the love of God.

I once knew, also, of a large manufactory in a Western city where an order was issued for the men to work on Sunday. After the morning service the pastor of a small church in the neighborhood called a meeting of his deacons to discuss the matter and see what action they could take. All sorts of suggestions were offered, but finally it was decided that they would let God use his own method for effecting the desired end; and for some days those Christian people met regularly and prayed that God would change the heart of that business man. By and by some of the members, who had been strengthened by their hours of communion and petition, went to the owner of the manufactory to speak with him regarding the matter. He replied that he had been thinking it over himself, and had decided that it would not be necessary to run the factory on the Sabbath.

Now notice the beautiful method of persuasion which God employs. He comes by his gospel to every man just where he is. He does not say to him, " Wait first until you see your faults and sins;" he does not say, " Wait until you are a better man;" but he comes to a man just wherever he finds him, and seeks to melt the hard heart, and appeals to the manliness not yet dead in his soul, and awakens visions and dreams of possibilities not yet vanished; and a new man is born—a new possession for the kingdom of God. A new power of righteousness is given to every man thus coming of his own free will; and because God has touched his heart he is born into the glorious liberty of the sons of God.

See, also, the blessed testimony this is to the truth. Think of that. It is easy for us to say that God is truth. It is easy for us to think that God knows all truth. It is easy for us to declare, one

to another, that religion is the method of truth.
But what is the proof of it? The proof lies outside of us and beyond anything in our plans. The
proof of all proofs lies in the divine method itself.
God has more at stake than we have, or than society has, or than the whole world taken together
has, in the success of his plan of redemption. God
has staked his own soul, we may reverently say,
upon saving the world, as the witness of his love.
He has done what divinity alone could conceive,
in the sacrifice of Jesus Christ.

What, then, does God do? He seems to stand
back and simply wait for the sure working of his
own plan. Now we judge men's integrity, we
judge their confidence in their own plans, by their
patience. Are they always trying to amend their
ways by doing something different? Ah! then
they are conscious of failure. Are they calm and
restful—steady in hand and method? Then they
believe in themselves. Through all the centuries
God has steadily proceeded with the uniform
method of revealing himself to men as the means
of their salvation—sending prophets, lawgivers,
divine messengers to tell men the truth, and in
the fullness of time sending his Son with more of
the truth of God; then leaving that truth to do
its own work.

Kepler, when he had discovered the wonderful
laws of astronomy, said, as he sent his book to

the press, " I can well wait a hundred years for a
reader, since God has waited six thousand years
for an observer." This is God's testimony to the
power of truth. How ample, how sure the words
when God's Word deals with the soul and its
needs! " Come unto me "—not you alone ; not
you who do not know temptation ; not you babe in
life who have not been harmed by the power of the
world ; not you philosopher, shielded in your school
from contact with the world as it is. " Come unto
me, all ye that labor and are heavy-laden "—bend-
ing under the crushing burden of your heart—
" and I will give you rest "—deliverance. That is
the divine method.

What, then, in conclusion ? Why, just see the
obligations that arise out of this! The greater
the privilege of our position the greater the re-
sponsibilities. The greater the love that is shown
the greater the abuse. What is the situation to-
day ? It is this : not the holy God appealing to
a world lying in darkness, but the holy God appealing to a world enlightened, self-respecting,
honest, upright ; affectionate men, good fathers,
good sons, loving mothers ; ladies who have honor
and dignity ; men with manliness for all the work
of life except God's work ; who have love and
kindness and generosity and patience for every
one and for everything in life except God ; who
open their hearts to all worldly interests that are

worthy, but close them against everything that
directly concerns God and his gospel. Think of
that! If this world, the world about us, should
heed, would not the degraded, the heathen world,
quickly be won?

Now you see what sin is, and the sin of "re-
spectable sin." This applies to young men
brought up in Christian homes, with all that
wealth and luxury and education and religion
can give to them, having enlightened minds for
everything that the world offers except God;
business men proud of their strength and their
dignity and force and citizenship; proud as fathers
and men and members of the community, but
having not one purpose of allegiance or of love
toward the Father in heaven, who has given to
you and is giving to you everything that you have
to enjoy. Think of this, not as the answer of
the heathen, not as the answer of the poor repro-
bate in the slums of the city, to a God whose names
even they have never heard except in curses; but
as the answer of men brought up in a Christian
atmosphere, sitting, as many of you do, Sabbath
after Sabbath, in a Christian church, to the God
who has been appealing to you all your lives in
the gentle, manly way of persuasion. What shall
we say of such a man? What remains for him
who has "counted the blood of the covenant
wherewith he was sanctified an unholy thing,"

and " has trodden underfoot " the offered gospel of his God? What more can God do? What remains? Is his truth not true?

It was my privilege this morning to pass in rapid review the twenty-five years in which I have been permitted to be a minister of the gospel; but who can put in words the experiences of those years, in the testimony that they have brought to the truth of Jesus Christ, in the home, on the sick-bed, by the open grave, in sorrow, in temptation, in pain, no less than in joy and in strength and success? The " great multitude whom no man can number "—young men and maidens, strong men and women, aged men to whom gray hairs have become a " crown of glory," because they are found in the way of righteousness—all uniting to bear testimony that Jesus Christ is to them life; that the gospel to them is true, and that no word of it has failed. Is the message not true?

And then as to the hearer—what more can be done? Men everywhere to-day say, " We are convinced; we are not infidels. Why, we have always believed the truth of the gospel." Yes, but you do nothing for the gospel. You must give yourself to the truth. You must repent; you must stop this life away from God and find your life in God. You must open your heart to respond to persuasion, and then it will come true, as I said at the beginning, that you will see manliness in being persuaded. There is no manliness in doubt. Doubt is paralysis. Delay in the face of the truth is weakness. God summons you— not to inquire, not to parley, not to talk about believing; God summons you every one, dear friends, to believe, and so to be saved. Will you not, then, recognize the truth? Will you not open your hearts to the graciousness of the divine method? Will you not regard the dignity of the appeal of the Lord Jesus Christ, and away with your unbelief, with your parleying, with your procrastination, and give yourself to the Lord Jesus Christ, and to his cause, with all your heart? Then shall you find peace, for then you shall find God.

X

IF A RELIGION, WHY NOT SOME OTHER?

" The glory of Christianity is, not to be as unlike other religions as possible, but to be their perfection and fulfilment."

DR. JOWETT OF BALLIOL.

" There is but one religion of which Renan could say, as he
says of the words of Jesus at the well, that if there were religion
in another planet it could be none other than this."

GOLDWIN SMITH, *Contemporary Review.*

" The difference between Christianity and all heathen religions
appears in the frequency with which their gods are changed.
The Zeus of Homer and of Plato are not only different, but an-
tagonistic in conception.   The gods of India are an endless pro-
cession.   The belief in Jesus Christ remains the same ; and the
last movement of Christian thought is the effort to go back more
certainly to the Jesus of the New Testament."

DR. JOWETT OF BALLIOL.

X

IF A RELIGION, WHY NOT SOME OTHER?

WE take up the question of the man who, being convinced of the need of a religion, asks, " Why must I accept the religion of Jesus Christ? There are many forms of religion and philosophy by which men who have discovered their need of something outside of themselves are assured that they can obtain what they need. Admitting that the way of Christ is deserving of the title by which it was known at the beginning—'the Way '—why should I regard it as the only way? Admitting that Jesus Christ is the Saviour of souls, why should I be taught that he is the only Saviour? There have always been earnest men in the world, and it seems to me that the same questions have been pressed on other hearts, certainly as sincere, and often quite as hard pushed as ourselves; and as the answers which they have received have lived through the centuries, why may not some of them do for us?" To these questions we ought to be able to give a definite answer. Certainly they are not new, and we ought to be able to find sufficient evidence in reply.

You may remember that there occurred in the Saviour's life an incident in which just this question was raised. The people had flocked about him, and, recognizing their needs, he had wrought the startling miracle of the feeding of the five thousand. The immediate effect was that the whole multitude was stirred with the conviction that he was truly the Messiah of Israel, and they ought to proclaim him their king then and there. The Saviour, seeing the emptiness of their faith, withdrew himself from them, and disappeared. The multitude, repelled by his unwillingness to accept their homage, left him, and many who had believed in him up to this time " followed him no more." His ministry began at once to fail, and failed continually until the end. It was then, in response to his saying to his disciples, " Will ye also go away?" that they turned to him with the inquiry, " Lord, to whom shall we go?" In making the choice which men to-day are making on every side they came with our question. It was a critical hour, and forced the conviction, " Thou hast the words of eternal life. And we believe and are sure that thou art that Christ the Son of the living God "—thou, and no one else.

Here were men who, passing through exactly this stage of inquiry, had reached a conclusion.

The multitude might go where they pleased; teachers more eloquent and more learned than they might instruct as they chose; but these men, unlettered and ignorant, if you will, had reached a conclusion that would remain with them through life. They were sure that they could be satisfied nowhere else in the world.

To see the reasons for their answer, and their sufficiency for us, we must spend a moment in considering what was the state of the world just at that time. On the one side of them was Egypt, that most wonderful of the ancient nations, with her striking testimony to some of the greatest truths that the mind of man has ever grasped. There stand to-day, as they stood then, her monuments—the pyramids and the Sphinx—proclaiming the faith of that people in the unseen, their abiding testimony to immortality in the life beyond the grave, and their conviction that the soul is to go on from life to life; that through all the forms in which they worshiped the unseen God they worshiped, not many gods, but rather only one. In other words, it was a very good counterpart of the philosophy or faith of the men who to-day, as agnostics, deny the sufficiency of any actual knowledge, whether of philosophy or of religion. They say that one may be as good as another; that all possess some truth; but, far beyond, there is something yet to be attained. For them the Sphinx stands as it stood to the Egyptians, the symbol of the unknown; in its person uniting the human and the animal; suggestive of the great fact that all life, however different its external forms, is essentially one; and that all knowledge, however distinctive it may be in certain relations, leads to the larger realm of truth yet unrevealed.

Egypt had borne her testimony through the centuries to portions of the truth, and yet Egypt was dead. Her place in history was to be vacant in the future; her religion had utterly failed.

Then, on the other hand, there were all the great forms of the Oriental religions. There was the testimony of India to the existence of a God, as the source and end of all being. In her testimony to the reality of the unseen she taught the law of self-discipline, of self-abnegation, and of the worthlessness of the things of this world in comparison with those of the world that is to be attained; and also the possibility of attaining that unseen world by one's personal effort. Gautama was a beautiful character, touched to his inmost soul by sorrow for sin, oppressed by human misery. But he knew no salvation for men from the sin he hated other than by annihilation. He would save men by destroying man; he magnified sin only, as has been said, that he might the more pour contempt on life. With all the loftiness of their aspirations, and the beauty of individual character, and the self-devotion which pictures the altruism that is the sum of religion in the minds of many to-day, all that Buddhism and Brahmanism could do for the world was India with her ignorance and superstition.

Then, nearer by, there were the Persians, who taught that there is an ever-present struggle in the world and in every human heart between good and evil. Now that is, to-day, the burden of thousands of anxious hearts. On every side are men who are crowded up against the evils of life, because society is corrupt, or because the laws are unjustly administered. They would destroy society, if need be; they would destroy the government, if need be; they would risk their own welfare, if need be, in order to start the world anew and escape this terrible outward pressure. We know these men to be wrong because their minds are centered on external rather than on internal evils. They would remake the world from without. But, after all, here is the recognition of the truth which every man finds in his own soul: there is an eternal conflict between good and evil, of which this world is the arena. Yet Zoroastrianism had no power to save the world. What has Persia to offer of a regenerated social order? Who would look to Persia for even a way of life?

Then there were the beautiful religions of Greece. Her message to the world was "the God of the present." Egypt had spoken of the possibilities of the future; India had spoken of the God of the unseen; and China had already talked, as she is talking to-day, of the God of the past—a past that the world had never seen, but a past whose dead hand destroyed for her the possibility of a future. But Greece, over against them all, had borne testimony to the God of the present. Her ideal was of a beauty greater than that which actually exists, and for which men continually strive. And Greece had thus testified that, whatever men may think of the future, there is that in the present which is worth living for. But with what result? Her very national life had vanished, her religion was forgotten, and nothing remained but the ruins of her literature and art, perishing already at home, to be preserved at last in other lands as the monuments of a vanished people, the most richly endowed the world has ever seen.

Then there were the Romans. As Greece stood for the men who pleaded for culture and refinement, for distinction in thought and bearing, and had failed—just as that form of culture fails to-day when dealing with the sins of the world —so Rome had now come on the field, with her splendid testimony to human brotherhood. She spread her wings over all peoples. She welcomed all gods, if only they would give their allegiance to the state. Contemporary with Paul was that " lame slave whom God loved "—a teacher of the truth—Epictetus; and later that Roman philosopher, Thraseas, who said he feared to hate sin lest he might be tempted to hate men; and that rare emperor, Marcus Aurelius, whose " Meditations," written for his own eyes, have been a consolation to human hearts ever since. And what had Rome done? Her own wise Lucretius told the truth when he spoke of religion as it was in his day as " lowering upon mortals with a hideous aspect, and pressing human life down under its inexorable foot." Her national life was already passing away. Her laws contained nothing of modern religion, and little or nothing of modern philosophy.

Most important of all the men of the Saviour's day were the Jews; that little nation so small that she had cut no figure among the nations of the world, and yet was destined to give to the world a Saviour.

What were some of the peculiar characteristics of this people? They believed in one God; and so had other nations. They had some views regarding the life beyond; but others had seemed to make much more of immortality. They had observed an external righteousness; others had

done the same. What, then, was the distinctive
message of Israel? It has been said that among
all the nations she alone pointed out the necessity of an inward life; the development of
the spiritual out of the carnal; and all her story
—the story of the Old Testament—turns about
this truth. In the Garden of Eden—the picture
to the Hebrew of the beginning of the human
race—the first man failed not because he grasped
at the tree of life, but because of an inward state
that led him to disobey. Abel was preferred
before Cain because his sacrifice was more acceptable as the offering of a docile and obedient
heart; and Jacob was preferred before Esau because in him the flesh was subordinate to the spirit.
And so on throughout the Old Testament. It
is the first-born who gives place to the second.
First the carnal, then the inward and spiritual, is
the great law of human existence. Jacob stands
before Esau; Joseph before his brethren; Samuel
before Saul; David before Jonathan; and so on
through the centuries. God says to us, " It is not
my power, it is not my knowledge; holiness, the
inward life, the conscience is my characteristic."
" Be ye holy; for I am holy." Take the law of
God, write it on the soul and life; joy and peace
and strength are to be found in walking in that
way. Now what was the result?

Men everywhere are saying that there is no

need of going to church, no need of cultivating
the spirit's life, no need of drawing near to God.
All you need is to do "what you think to be
right." What was the outcome of this plan with
the Jews, in their degeneracy; with their scribes
and Pharisees, and their readiness to slay the
prophets? It is the plan which the world has
been trying ever since, while darkness and despair
have settled down upon men from the highest to
the lowest, until finally the question comes to be
asked, "Lord, to whom shall we go?" It is the
question of many a burdened heart to-day. What
is the answer? "Thou hast the words of eternal
life." No one else has. "And we know, we believe and are sure, that thou art the Son of the
living God." There is no one else who can bring
God down to us or lift us up to God.

Now why is it? Because every heart has the
same needs. There is the need of pardon; the
need of deliverance from our own past, with its
guilt, and from our own present, with its weakness
and its ignorance; the revelation of ourselves to
ourselves, with the promise of a better self. And
the Lord Jesus Christ brought all this when he
came into our life; being born as we are born,
and giving himself to our daily experiences.
Coming into the humblest needs of the plainest
man, not seeking the wise or the pure or the upright, but everywhere the publicans and sinners

(for whom the religions of the world and the philosophers of the world had no place), he reveals the Heavenly Father as seeking the souls that are his, and that were lost.

Now the life of Jesus Christ is the one sufficient life for the world because it comes to men in their deepest needs. It shows to every man his own true nature, his lost estate, and then reveals to him the true life of the soul which is to be found nowhere else.

In all our lives there are two or three simple but universal needs. We all have a sense of dependence; we cannot save ourselves. We all have a sense of brotherhood; we want to know God and be found in him, and in such a way that our friends and neighbors may find him with us. And then we all have the desire of progress—the possibility of doing better; we want to be better men and better women; we want to grow in grace and in the knowledge of God. And nothing will satisfy us unless it meets these three conditions. The Lord Jesus Christ, coming down into our lives, has opened to us access to the Father. We all receive our life from him. We have grieved him by our sins, and yet his love is so great that he has not cast us out, but now, even now, he has called us to himself, to grow up in his love, and to be his henceforth and forever. The tasks which are given us he will help us to

perform, and he will be with us " alway, even unto
the end of the world."

And so the Lord Jesus Christ comes to men
who are burdened with their sins, weighed down
by care, depressed by sorrow; and what is the
message which he brings to every man? " Be
my disciple." " Begin the new life now, and a
new heaven shall be begun in you, and shall then
spread to those about you." It tells of a heaven
to begin now; that has commenced already in the
heart of every man who gives himself to the Lord
Jesus Christ. The Saviour said, " My peace I
give unto you "—a peace to be realized by every
guilty, sin-burdened soul; the world cannot give
such peace, and cannot take it away. And then
he comes opening infinite growth for the soul in
" the glorious liberty of the sons of God."

It is this promise of God—to meet all our needs
—which we find nowhere else. He has proved
himself the Saviour of a great multitude whom no
man can number, out of all nations and kindreds
and tongues and people, in all the centuries; and
there are to-day, in all parts of the world, men
who can stand up and bear testimony to the truth
that God does indeed meet and satisfy all their
needs, and to the glorious assurance of a home
with him in the life to come.

So that in answer to the question, If a religion,
why not some other? we can say that all others

have failed. Whatever of truth there was in any one of them is to be found in its fullest expression in the religion of Christ. All that men can long for is to be had in Christ. All that other religions have contributed to the best thought and the best learning and the best life of the world is reproduced in the religion of the Lord Jesus Christ, and in that new setting has gained what it never had before. " I am the Light of the world," said the Saviour, and we see that light realized. " I am the Way "—the world has sadly proved there is no other. " I am the Life"; and the world has found nowhere else the life of God—nowhere except in Jesus Christ. Therefore every man who craves life; every man who longs for fellowship with the Father; every man whose soul is stirred for brotherhood with his fellows; every man who would know himself and gain strength to overcome himself, will find all he needs in the faith as it is in Jesus.

XI

WHAT IS FAITH?

" Faith is a living, reasonable confidence in the grace of God; so certain that it would die upon such grounds a thousand times over."   LUTHER.

" The Christian life is begun, so far as man's part in it is concerned, in the entrance of the soul into a right relation to God, and is perpetuated in the constancy and increasing closeness of that relation.   Man's part in the constitution of this relation is faith, and his part in the continuance and strengthening of it continues to be faith. . . . Faith is not a mere confidence that a work of grace will be done for us, but a consent that a work of grace shall be wrought in us.   The power of faith thus resides, not in its exercise, as if it were an achievement, but in its object, because it is a personal relation of one who is helpless and dependent to Christ, who is able to save and purify."
STEVENS, " Pauline Theology," p. 298.

XI

WHAT IS FAITH?

THIS question of faith lies at the very heart of religion; it also lies at the heart of a religious life. The question, then, is not at all theoretical; it is the most practical with which any of us can be engaged. That it is a question worthy of somewhat careful thought, as being indeed a question of modern inquiry, is suggested by the fact that not very long ago an intelligent and educated gentleman, brought up in a Christian home, and in the habit of attending church all his life, said to me in a thoughtful way, "I wish you would tell me just what you mean by faith."

Of course it is easy to answer the query in the ordinary terms of common speech. We say that faith is " to believe." But why is faith the center and heart of religion; and why is it true that "without faith it is impossible to please" God; and why is it that from the beginning, through all the long Christian centuries, with all their varieties of Christian belief, the definition of faith has always been a central and burning one in theological discussion?

In attempting to answer this question use is
made of two equally erroneous definitions. One
is this: " Faith is the acceptance of a proposition
on the ground of confidence in the person stating
it." It is receiving testimony from another as
being credible wholly apart from any consideration of what the testimony itself may be. This
is the definition of John Locke, one of the most
powerful thinkers in the English-speaking world,
a man who has done more to mold the thoughts
of subsequent generations than almost any other
mind. But the definition is incomplete in that it
places faith on an unsubstantial foundation ; it
exalts authority ; it offers no evidence other than
the word of the witnesses ; it stakes everything
on a report, on a record, on a statement. The
result is that it leads to an idolatry of the book,
and only raises new difficulties in the way of those
who are unwilling to receive any testimony
merely on the word of men like themselves. It
has resulted in laying stumbling-blocks in the way
of some, and in leading others to a faith which
rests only upon the word of some religious teacher ;
in some communities it has exalted creeds into final
and authoritative statements ; and it always tends
to lure souls to intellectual, if not to spiritual sleep,
because the church once for all has defined for
them what they are to believe.

Another definition, quite the opposite of this,

is that faith is " belief in what is proved." That
is the definition of people who exalt the reason.
It stands as the justification of what we are accus-
tomed to define as " rationalism." It is the warrant for what is called " liberal" Christianity—that
is, a breaking free from the dominating beliefs
of others. Early in the century, Dr. Channing,
one of the broadest and most intelligent of men,
prophesied that there would be great value in
erecting this conception of religious faith as a bul-
wark against infidelity. But he lived to see his
mistake; it has always disappointed its advocates.
The truth is that in all the work of life we have
to walk by faith in things not proved. Sir William
Herschel says that three sevenths of the moon's
surface is always hidden from our sight, however
powerful the instruments which we may use to
help us see. We have to act without provable
knowledge of what is there; and life goes on.

Man is not merely a reasoning animal. He is
a seeing, feeling, contemplating, acting animal, as
Cardinal Newman has said; and in this catalogue
of man's characteristics the power of reason is
only one among others—a significant, an essential
one, if you will, and yet one that is sharply limited. The testimony of the centuries has always
been that faith has its roots, not in man's intellect, not in his powers of reason simply, but in all
parts of his being. There is that within a man,

hidden somewhere, lying close to that which is
the very essence of himself, to which religion
speaks, and out of which faith springs. Religion
is, in the last analysis, an appeal to the deepest
needs of every man; and therefore the question
must be, What are man's deepest needs? Before
we can know what religion is, before we can know
what faith is, we must know what that is in man
which religion comes to satisfy.

When we come, then, to inquire as to what our
needs are, we are confronted at once with the fact
that it is hard to discover. We look into our
own hearts and we discover that things are not as
they should be. We find that we cannot even
read our own character aright. We cannot clearly
understand, still less interpret, our own motives.
We are very complex creatures. We carry in our
hearts the effects of all our past experiences—
our temptations, our weaknesses. Before we
can know ourselves truly we shall need to find a
standpoint outside of ourselves, and to look down
upon ourselves as the angels look down from
heaven. How can any one measure sin, for example, when he himself is not moved with sorrow
for his own wrong-doing? How can he measure
the effect of weakness of the will in yielding to
temptation, how can he know the meaning of
remorse, when he has never known the meaning
of his own guilt? How can any man know the

needs of his own soul, when he has not been able
to take in the length and breadth and height and
depth of his own divinely created nature? And
yet, under all these limitations, we must ask,
" What are our deepest needs? " When we look
into our own hearts these are some of the things
we find :

Every man finds that he has a conscience;
often dulled and hardened, and yet never, surely,
destroyed. Every man is warned by it of the
seriousness of wrong-doing. It keeps before his
mind a sense of guilt; it brings shame; and it
awakens at times the sense of fear. As the Scripture puts it, " The wicked flee when no man
pursueth : but the righteous are bold as a lion."
Why do they flee? They flee because of their
own thoughts; for back of their thoughts there lies
the idea of a judge. We feel in our souls the need
of being set right before the ultimate tribunal.
Conscience makes cowards of us all.

Then we all have a sense of dependence. We
have not called ourselves into being. We can
make our plans for the future, but we are aware
that we cannot extend the boundaries of our
lives. In the words of the Scripture, we cannot
add one cubit to the length of our days. We are
as " the grass of the field, which to-day is, and
to-morrow is cast into the oven." " The wind
passeth over it, and it is gone; and the place

thereof shall know it no more." The nations that were before us are gone—all of them—and the men of to-day will be gone to-morrow; and we are all dependent upon something without ourselves.

And this sense of dependence is real, and not merely theoretical. There are voices in the heart that cry as a child cries in the night. We do not know what we need, but still there is a sense of need with us all. We seem to live as in a void. We may be in the midst of a multitude, and yet we dwell alone. "The heart knoweth his own bitterness; and a stranger doth not intermeddle with his joy."

Every man discovers, as he searches his own heart, this sense of dependence; and then as we search we discover, also, that we have a capacity for being something better than we now are. In other words, we all have a capacity for progress. We call it, sometimes, the dream of youth. We lose these dreams as we grow older; but hidden deep within the heart there is still the possibility of being greater and wiser and better than we are. The psalmist says, " As the hart panteth after the water-brooks, so panteth my soul after thee, O God." The thought of God brings to us the thought of a purity better than our own, of a holiness vaster, higher, more profound than anything that we know, and of a Divinity from whom we came and into whose enfolding love we would again be taken; and realizing this, we are conscious that we have powers within us for which, in the service of One greater and wiser and better than we are, we should find employment.

And then we find—all of us—a consciousness of weakness before temptation. Paul's words are our words: " The good that I would, I do not: but the evil which I would not, that I do." We are all aware that the power of the will is the noblest faculty God has given us, and yet somehow that power slips from us. We cannot hold it to its duty. And every man longs for power over himself—longs for the ability to come off victor in that battle which is always being waged about the citadel of the soul.

Now, with this survey of the needs that come with an awakened conscience, and a consciousness of dependence, and a longing to be better, and the desire for an established will that shall hold firmly and steadily to the right, we hear the voice of religion. The voice comes to us from without. It calls us to live a life different from that which we are living. We have an instance in the case of the Roman jailer who was keeper of the prison in which Paul and Silas were confined. He was aware that there were needs in his own heart, but, like us, he had been able to live on from day to day, hushing or neglecting them. Suddenly he thought of the difference between himself and the prisoners, who, with their feet in the stocks, were singing songs of praise; and the conviction came to him that they were not dependent upon outward surroundings or circumstances for their happiness. Then we hear him crying out, " Sirs, what must I do to be saved?"

We cry, " Who can show us any good?" Who can bring to us what will satisfy, not hunger, not thirst, not a longing for success in business; but who shall satisfy for us the deeper needs of the soul?—these needs which come to us all, men and women alike; and just as really to men and women who have lived honored by all as to the vilest outcast on the street. " Sirs, what must I do to be saved"—from what I have been; from what I am; from what I may become? Now comes the answer: " Believe on the Lord Jesus Christ, and thou shalt be saved."

It is the answer of men who have themselves been saved; and without stopping to think out an extended and confusing reply to the query, they at once give answer, in the words we have quoted, to the needs which have sprung up in this man's heart. Faith is that acceptance of God which the soul is capable of putting forth when it is conscious of its own needs and learns that God has come to meet those needs.

Just on this point John Bunyan tells his experience. He says that he had been for a long time in great distress on account of his sins, and that in some way there fell into his hands a little book, so old and worn that he could hardly keep it together long enough to read it. It was Luther on Paul's Epistle to the Galatians; and that plain tinker began to read. He says, " I found my condition in his experience so largely and profoundly handled as if his book had been written out of my heart." That is the experience of every man who comes to the Bible in the same spirit. He finds that his needs are handled so largely and profitably in one part or another of God's Word that he might think it had been written out of his own heart.

John Wesley, after calling himself a Christian for some time, fell in with some plain German Pietists in London, who put in his hands Luther's preface to Paul's Epistle to the Romans; and the result of his reading was exactly what it was in the case of Bunyan in reading the Epistle to the Galatians. From that moment a new light came into his soul. He had been trying to fit himself for God, when suddenly he became aware that God himself was dealing with the deepest needs of his soul ; that God's method of dealing with those needs was sufficient ; and that all he had to do was to commit himself to the hand of his Saviour, and trust in him fully, and him only, for salvation.

You see that this is an appeal to all man's powers. It is not an appeal to the reason only. It is an appeal to all that is good in us to be given to God. It is a worthy appeal because it consecrates all a man's powers to the service of God. Therefore the result is that faith at once frees a man from his old life. What is the old life? It is the life that any man leads who has not known the truth. He feels a longing for a bettering of himself which he cannot obtain. His will is weak. Now all that old life is laid aside; what he cannot do God has come to do for him; he leaves his old life behind, just as he would an old garment when he has his new suit to put on. And so faith not only enables us to throw the old life off, but it makes the new life a reality.

How full the world is of testimony to this truth! Faith reveals itself and proves itself by works. Indeed, it proves itself in two ways. " The Spirit itself beareth witness with our spirit, that we are the children of God." If a child is lost, and you find it, and say, " I know the way ; I will lead you home," that child is no longer afraid. He trusts you to do as you have promised. So it is with a lost soul. When found, he is " safe in the arms of Jesus," and at peace. God has found him, and he knows it.

But not only is there peace in the heart, there is also witness of faith in the life; for the man that has been found by God proves it by the life that he lives. Like the child that has been lost, he no longer walks in his own way, but in the way of Him who is leading him back. Faith is the putting of all one's being in God's hands as in the hands of a faithful Creator, asking, "What must I do to be saved?" "Believe on the Lord Jesus Christ, and thou shalt be saved," is the answer that gives both the method and the result. Recognize that the Lord knows the guilt of a guilty conscience; that he knows the longings of a hungering and thirsting heart; that he has come to seek and to save that which was lost; and that he has come, "not to call the righteous, but sinners to repentance." Believe, and thou shalt live.

That was the method in Paul's day. It was witnessed in the lives of the new Christians, and commented upon by the heathen about them. They saw that these men who but now were prodigals and outcasts were changed. Their faith attested itself in their lives. The witness was triumphant. And if any man to-day asks, "What must I do to be saved?" the answer of the church to him, the answer of every Christian soul out of the fullness and gladness of its own personal experience, is not, "First try to make yourself better;" not, "Search for Christian evi-

dences;" but simply, "Believe on the Lord Jesus
Christ. Lift up your heart and your hands to
him. Cry out to him for pardon, and for peace
and grace and strength, and it is given; and then
go on your way to live for him." And none that
ever so came to him was cast out.

XII

THE TRUTH ABOUT PRAYER

" More things are wrought by prayer
Than this world dreams of."

TENNYSON, " Morte d'Arthur."

" Prayer is the greatest power in the world—it keeps us near
to God.   My own prayer has been most weak, wavering, incon-
stant, but it has been the best thing I ever did.   I think this a
universal truth."   GENERAL S. C. ARMSTRONG.

" God, the only good of all intelligent natures, is not an absent
or a distant God, but is more present in and to our souls than
our own bodies ; and we are strangers to heaven and without God
in the world for this only reason : because we are void of that
spirit of prayer which can alone unite, and never fails to unite us
with the one only God, and to open heaven and the kingdom of
God within us."

WILLIAM LAW, " The Spirit of Prayer."

" O my dear friend, to pray ; to pray as God would have us ;
to pray with all the heart and strength, with the reason and the
will; to believe vividly that God will listen to your voice through
Christ, and verily do the thing he pleaseth thereupon—this is the
last, the greatest achievement of the Christian's warfare on earth.
Teach us to pray, O Lord!"   COLERIDGE.   Letter to a friend.

174

XII

THE TRUTH ABOUT PRAYER

THERE is no Christian habit upon which modern thought bears in opposition more positively than this of prayer. There is no matter of Christian belief concerning which we all need to be more definitely convinced. A practice that meant so much to the Saviour ought to mean much to us. When we open the Bible we see that prayer was the fixed habit of the Saviour's life. He began with prayer, he continually turned aside to the mountains or to the desert to pray, he sometimes spent the whole night in prayer; and of the few facts that are recorded of him there is none to which such frequent reference is made as this.

In his most exalted moments, as on the Mount of Transfiguration, he did not omit it; and in the supreme hour in the Garden of Gethsemane he withdrew alone to pray. His last words on the cross were a prayer.

When we turn to his disciples we observe at once this habit as being also characteristic of them. The fact that any man prayed was already rec-

ognized as a sign that God's Spirit had taken
possession of his heart. " Behold, he prayeth,"
was the comforting assurance to the believers in
Damascus concerning the enemy Saul.   And as
we read the exhortations of those early Christians in the Epistles, we find everywhere constant
emphasis put upon the necessity and privilege of
prayer.   We are " always to pray," we are to
" pray without ceasing "; " in everything by
prayer and supplication with thanksgiving " we
are to let our requests be made known unto God ;
and there is much illustration of the method of
prayer.

The question arises, What is prayer?   And the
answer that comes to our thought is that " prayer
is the act by which a man, conscious at once of
his weakness and of his immortality, puts himself
into effective communication with God."   It is
to be an effective communication—one which will
meet his needs in the wants both of his heart and
of his life.

It is this act of the heart of man reaching out
toward God, and seeking to lay permanent hold
upon God, to get into enduring and effective re-
lationship with God, which has characterized religion in all ages and in all conditions of life,
whatever may be the form of worship.   However
degraded the religion of the heathen, or however
elevated the religion of the philosopher, prayer is

its abiding characteristic. And this would seem
to be the universal experience; for when left to
themselves men instinctively express themselves
in some form of prayer. That acute Greek philosopher, Plutarch, said, " You may travel in all
lands, you may find men without letters and
without art; but you will never find them
without altars, without ceremonials, and without
prayer."

Accepting this, then, as the great outward fact
coextensive with religion, we recognize that it is
a work in which religion engages all the strength
of a man's nature. Everything in the world that
is worthy, that gets a hold upon men, advances
in the respect which men have for it by the extent to which it gathers up all the forces of their
being and makes them tributary to its service.
Those things which touch only a part of our nature—the passing thought, the mere whim, the
incidental affection—are the things which we treat
as trivial in our lives; but when, now and again,
we are confronted with some thought or power
which challenges our entire being, then, at once,
we are arrested. This, also, is the characteristic
of religion as it reveals itself in prayer.

Prayer is an act. It begins in adoration. It
is the summons that comes to a man out of his
heart, or from what he has been taught in worship, calling him to bring himself to the foot of

the throne of God to render to God a fitting adoration, to enlarge his thought in the presence of the divine, to prepare himself to understand the Almighty, and in so doing to get some understanding of his own origin, nature, and destiny.

But not only does religion summon man in prayer to use his intellect, it also summons him to use his heart, because adoration without affection is idle, and one who takes upon himself to pray, with some understanding of the meaning of that act, challenges his soul to feel in some measure the thought which is given to him of his Maker and of himself. And as his thoughts turn inward from his first conception of God, he begins to measure his own needs, his weaknesses and temptations, and his own possibilities, his emotions are kindled, and he longs to feel as well as to know.

But, after all, this is only the external truth concerning prayer. We do not get at its real essence until we seek to know God's thoughts and to understand God's love, in order that we may give ourselves to some definite service, in order that we may summon our souls to do what the thoughts and emotions of the hour impel us to do. Thus the essence of prayer is importunity—" I will not let thee go, except thou bless me." It is shown in the parable of the unjust judge granting the prayer of the widow because of the urgency of her petition. The conception of God as the one great source of supply for all man's needs has been given to the heart. The thought has penetrated so far into the depths of a man's nature that he cannot be satisfied with anything short of this. He must cry out after God until the answer comes, that he may be at peace. Therefore prayer must be something more than unuttered aspiration or longing awakened in a man's soul. It must be the gathering together of all the powers of his being, and then the concentrating of them upon the one purpose of laying hold upon God, to know as he is known, and to love as he is loved. Something like this is the first effort of prayer. Because a man comes from God he seeks to enter into effective communion with God.

Then the question rises, Is all this of any use? What is the effect of prayer? What is the bottom truth in regard to this almost universal habit of mankind? There can be no question as to some of the effects of prayer; for example, those effects which are to be observed in a man's own life. When a man is known to be a praying man we recognize that the wavering man gains strength and stability; that the selfish man rises above his selfishness; that the irascible man secures self-control; in short, that the habit of prayer proves itself potent in a man's heart and life. Then, also, it is true that prayer has certain

of what may be called social effects, so that, as
some one has well said, " No man can think lightly
of one for whom he habitually prays." We may
cultivate thoughts of kindness toward a person;
but when we begin to pray regularly and earnestly
for him, then he enters into an entirely new relation to our life, and it becomes impossible for us
to think lightly of him, still less to be indifferent
to his welfare.

So in all the relations of daily life. Tenderness
springs from prayer; cheerfulness, hopefulness,
in short, the humanizing of the heart and life, and
the building up of a life in which character
broadens and sweetens as the days go by.

But the real question arises when we come to
prayer in its upward relations—in our intercourse
with God. What is prayer in that direction? It
is manifestly peace; it is adoration; it is the upward turning of that in a man's heart which en-
nobles the man himself in his thoughts of the unseen and eternal, whether he knows that there
is a God or not. Indeed, wholly apart from the
proofs of the existence of God, there is that which
makes a man conscious that he is rising into his
best estate when he is seeking to enter into the
thoughts of One who is above and superior to
him.

But the insistent question is, Does prayer bring
answer? Is there any direct communion between

the suppliant and the Creator? Is there any
special method by which God answers prayer?
We are confronted by what is said on every
side about natural law. And we are at once
compelled to ask, "What is natural law?" In
the earlier stages of man's intelligence all the ordinary phenomena of nature are interpreted as
so many manifestations of the unseen powers
that dwell in the heavens; but as man's knowledge increases he knows that the forces of electricity and of light are but ways in which the laws
of God reveal themselves. If, at the beginning,
we conceive of nature as dominated by a material
force that is self-existent and self-sustaining, then
there is no room for God in the universe, and
there is no possible place for prayer; but when
we inquire of nature concerning force we find
nowhere evidence that there is such God-exclud-
ing force. We find that force is revealed in a
long series of effects which are more or less uniform. We say they are the result of natural law.
And for all the practical purposes of life that observation is adequate; but in the last analysis we
are compelled to find some origin for force back
of nature. Therefore we must seek some other
interpretation of nature; and then the question
arises, Did God, at the beginning, in creating the
universe, determine its methods of action, wind
it up, and start it to running along certain fixed

lines? In that case he has limited himself; put himself out of nature, if not out of existence. He would be like the manufacturer of some great and complicated machine which, having made, he must leave to take care of itself, lest, if he interfere with it, it might destroy itself and him.

How, then, is nature related to God? He called it into being and he sustains it in being. So far as we have been able to observe his methods, in certain directions we have discovered what we call " uniformity." In other words, God has condescended to let us read his thoughts and understand his ways in certain directions, just as some electrician or engineer might invite us into his workshop, and, knowing well the limitations of our knowledge, might condescend to explain a certain machine in his possession, and we would reveal our excitement and pleasure as we grasped the principles of its construction; but we would not imagine for a moment that we knew as much about it as he who invented it.

Now, like that is the divine method in nature. God has revealed certain ways of working which we call the laws of nature, which had a beginning, and which may have an end, but which for the time being mark the attention of the divine Hand. What is there in all the universe that prevents God from acting in accord with these methods and still answering prayer? We pray to him for the safe return of a friend who is on the sea. The ship which the friend is in may be driven by the wind; but other elements are working with the wind—the captain who sets the sails and looks after the crew, the pilot who determines the course—these and a thousand other forces all may work together in answer to the prayer we breathe. All these powers are made to conform to the divine will; are, indeed, but the movement of the divine will in response to the need of God's child.

So in all the relations of life. We expect, we believe, that God is able to answer our call for spiritual blessings. We know that he is more willing to give than we are to ask. But not more sure is his gift of the Spirit than is his gift of food for the body. All the forces of nature are alike but the unfolding of his will, working together to bring out what he purposes; thus nature is but the expression of the ever-present Creator, the bountiful Father leading his child through the vast machinery in the great manufactory of earth, and using it all daily and hourly to bless those whom he loves. This, then, is the true answer of nature to the cry of man seeking communion with his Maker. At once the world becomes the instrument of God to be used in doing his will.

In the opening sentence of the prayer which the Saviour put on the disciples' lips we are taught to

say, " Our Father which art in heaven. . . . Thy
kingdom come. Thy will be done." All prayer,
then, should be under those conditions. We do
not wait to see whether the particular prayer is
answered. The child has found its Father; and
now, having found him, having worshiped him,
having felt his love in the heart, and having been
kindled with his thoughts, the creature commits
himself to his Creator; the child finds peace in
being in his Father's house.

Does he get an answer to his prayer so that he
knows it? Certainly! The answer comes with
the prayer. He feels that he has found God; and
whether or not God gives him the specific thing
he asks, he gives him his blessing. Whatever
the Father gives he accepts as blessing; what the
Father reveals he accepts as the Father's will;
and he prays always as the Saviour has taught us
to pray—" Not my will, but thine, be done."

Now as to the result of this knowledge of our
relation to God. We find, as Canon Liddon has
said, that " prayer is what prevents religion from
degenerating into mere religious thought on the
one side, or into mere philanthropy on the other."
Prayer is what exalts sentiment into action and
service to humanity into worship. It is, as I
said at the beginning, the summoning of all man's
nature to gain effective communion with God, and
then to carry that sense of God's presence into all

one does and thinks in daily life. Prayer, then, is indispensable to us all; for we all have to seek the face of God. It is not alone the privilege of the recluse, shut out from the world. It is the means which God has given us, and to which we come instinctively, for finding God, for living with him, and for carrying about with us a sense of his presence, deriving from it comfort and peace and calmness and strength.

As we look back along the line of Old Testament heroes we see that David and Samuel, Elijah and Daniel, and all the prophets were men who prayed; and in their praying they laid effective hold upon God, and God revealed himself not only to them, but through them; and through them the world became conscious of God's presence.

"O thou that hearest prayer," is the cry of the psalmist, "unto thee shall all flesh come." Why? Because all men are born of God and must needs find God. "I love the Lord, because he hath heard my voice and my supplications. Because he hath inclined his ear unto me, therefore will I call upon him as long as I live." That is the testimony of a heart that has found God for itself, and that is the enduring answer of the Christian to the world in all its questionings as to the reality of the Christian's prayer.

When life draws to its close we shall all be sure to find that we have wasted many of its precious

hours. We have wasted them in our work in doing things that were trivial; we have wasted them
in our study upon things that were but passing;
in pleasures which even at the time we knew were
unsatisfying. We shall then discover that we used
best that time which we consecrated to finding
God in prayer. The men who, as Christians,
have done the greatest work for Christ in the
world were the men who prayed. Calvin was
the man of one book, the man who walked with
God; John Wesley had great power in prayer;
and Luther often said, " Because I am crowded
with work to-day, I must spend more time than
usual in prayer."

So for us all, dear friends, if we are to be
Christians indeed, if we are to do God's work in
the world, we must call upon our souls and all
that is within us—we must summon the best
energies of our life—until we too have laid enduring hold upon the throne of grace. When we can
say, " I have called upon the Lord, and he has
heard my prayer," then, and not until then, are
we at peace.

XIII

A SAVIOUR FROM SIN

"I am sure that there are many persons who believe in Christ, who come to him and accept the salvation he offers, but who stop there, and whose life flickers and almost goes out for their want of realizing the position to which they are called. It is when we abide in Christ every moment, as the branch in the vine; when we surrender all to him and lie in his arms; and when we look on salvation not as a thing we are to touch and then have done with, or occasionally recall to mind, but a real, living, constant union with Christ in thought, in will and object—it is thus indeed that we have peace and calm and assurance and life."

LETTER FROM LORD CAIRNS SHORTLY
BEFORE HIS DEATH.

XIII

A SAVIOUR FROM SIN

THE distinctive feature of Christianity is that it offers salvation, not through theology, nor through a ritual, nor through a discipline of life, but by a personal Saviour. In this respect it is different from all other forms of faith. The appeal that is made in the gospel is not simply, "Come into a better life," nor, "Come into the acceptance of a definite truth," nor, "Come into a particular form of worship," but, "Come unto me, and live." The one who thus addresses us is Jesus Christ, and the story of his life is the story of the divine condescension: God in the person of his Son coming down into our life—born as we are born; laboring as men labor; meeting temptation in all points as we are tempted, yet without sin; understanding our sorrows and sicknesses, bearing them upon his own heart; and at last going down voluntarily into the grave, and being raised from the dead to prove the fullness of the life that is in him; and then, from the standpoint of a risen Saviour, proclaiming his

189

abiding presence in the world henceforth. This
is the gospel—the "good news" to men—from
the lips of him who accomplished it; and now
through his Word and his followers' testimony the
world is to be saved.

The question then arises, How does this
Saviour accomplish salvation for sinners? The
New Testament is the unfolding of that truth.
It does not announce a thesis which it proceeds
to prove. It sets before us a series of pictures—
suggestions—as to the way in which God finds
access to a sinful heart, and then by his own
power leads that heart out of helplessness into
strength, out of despair into hope, out of bondage
into " the glorious liberty of the sons of God."

In order to make that truth real, reference is
frequently had to the Old Testament ritual, the
sacrifices, and the law; and yet the Saviour, coming to redeem the world, does not offer himself
after the fashion of the Old Testament offering.
He comes to set the law aside; to declare that it
has been an imperfect instrument, valuable chiefly
as a symbol of the work which he is to accomplish. He comes to establish a new covenant in
himself.

We have the Saviour presenting himself as a
" great high priest "—using the figure of the high
priest of the Old Testament, who entered alone
into the holy of holies once a year, and there

obtained remission of the sins of the people. But not as such a priest or mediator did Jesus come. If he had he would, of necessity, have had to remain on earth forever; his work would have been incessant. He came to accomplish what a high priest could not do. He secures a redemption which no ritual and no sacrifice and no service, under the most favorable conditions, could accomplish for a sinful heart. "What the law could not do, in that it was weak," he has done. What the blood of bulls and of goats could not accomplish, he has come to perfect. When John saw the Saviour he exclaimed, "Behold, the Lamb of God, which taketh away the sin of the world!" In the ritual of the Old Testament it was not a lamb that was offered for sin, but a bullock or a goat. John undoubtedly gets his figure from the fifty-third chapter of Isaiah, where the Coming One is "brought as a lamb to the slaughter, and as a sheep before her shearers is dumb, so he openeth not his mouth." "He was wounded for our transgressions, he was bruised for our iniquities," that he might accomplish once for all the redemption which every soul needs. The high priest went into the holy of holies ceremonially fitted to make atonement for the sins of the people. This new Saviour is without sin; he alone thinks God's thoughts and feels as God feels and is one with the Father; and

he alone has condescended to plead for the sinner
with that love which knows no change or weariness, evermore saying, " Come unto me, and ye
shall find rest unto your souls."

The work that this Saviour of sinners has accomplished is a redemptive work—a " ransom-
ing " work, as the word so often is. " He gave
himself for us," to take the place of one who is
under bondage.   We see this Saviour coming out
of that unlimited life that lies beyond the veil,
and coming into this narrow life in which we are
found, that he may bear our burdens and share
our sorrows and experience our temptations;
doing all this of his own free will, in order that
in so doing he may win the right to bear us upon
his own heart before the throne of the Judge
of the universe ; and doing all with the full assurance that his prayers shall be heard.

He alone has access to the throne of grace ; he
alone has the right to secure redemption to those
who are under the bondage of sin ; and that " not
without blood," for his own blood was offered
freely as the proof of the divine Messiahship ;
and with this as a witness to his right to be the
Redeemer, he draws near to God.

Now notice that in all human sacrifices there
is the desire to appease an angry God.   All that
is swept aside by the coming of the Saviour.
He comes from the Father ; and when he has

revealed the Father, and has accomplished the
Father's will, he turns back to the arms of the
Father, which are open to receive him. The
gates of death are thrown aside, that he might
win a victory and be enabled to save men from
their sins.

We come then to this as the great central truth
in the work of this new Redeemer. This Saviour,
who has been sent from the Father, and who has
done all this, comes with a message for all men
everywhere. It is either for all men or for none.
He comes not to call the righteous, but sinners to
repentance. He comes to seek and to save that
which was lost. He comes to reveal the love of
the Father, not in proportion as he sees that
there is more righteousness in some hearts than
in others, but to reveal that righteousness which
no wickedness in any man's heart has interfered
with or destroyed. He comes to reveal that
Heavenly Father who, because he loves as no
man can love, can reveal in his Son a redemption
such as man cannot know.

There we have the personal Saviour first calling men by his own voice, and then calling them
by his message of redemption. "He is able also to
save them to the uttermost that come unto God
by him." No individual has been so great a sinner but that the Saviour who speaks to him can
lead him into life. Then what he does for one

he does for all, that all men everywhere may find life. "The blood of Jesus Christ his Son cleanseth us from all sin." "This is a faithful saying," says Paul, again and again, "and worthy of all acceptation, that Christ Jesus came into the world to save sinners."

This redemption which was in the personal Saviour becomes effective when we heed his invitation and open our hearts to his coming; when we hear him say, "Come unto me and live." Men do not know this; therefore the need of preaching the gospel. Therefore the Lord prayed for his servants, " I pray not that thou shouldest take them out of the world, but that thou shouldest keep them from the evil." " Ye are my witnesses." Tell men of the personal Saviour, with an individual message to every man and every woman, however lost in darkness, however hardened in heart or weighed down with care.

I remember, not long ago, seeing an account of some miners who were entombed by an explosion. The rescuing-party discovered that they were still alive, and then set to work with all possible despatch to save them. Day after day the reliefs worked, until they broke through the last foot of rock that separated them from the imprisoned miners, who were at the last gasp. Then it was discovered that the rescuers had not done all the work; for the imprisoned miners had heard the sound of the tools, and had strenuously, though feebly, set to work to meet them. While the relief-party had cut perhaps forty or fifty feet, they had gone but five or six; yet that had been just enough to complete their deliverance. If they had not done their part, small as it was, they would have perished.

So, many men seem to think that this divine Saviour is now working for us; he is tunneling through the hard rock of the world's obduracy, and if we are to be saved we must be working toward him, because our salvation depends upon what we may do to supplement his work.

All this is a mistake, and leads us to wonder why our hearts are so hard, and why we are not better Christians, instead of knowing that the loving Saviour has come to us himself, as a father goes to seek his lost child, and discovering him takes him up in his arms and carries him back to his home, doing all that needs to be done to save him that was lost; and all we have to do is to welcome the Saviour and commit to him the keeping of our souls, as a little child commits himself to his father who has found him.

This is the message which God has given us to-day of the Saviour from sin. You see why faith in this Saviour, who came to us himself, bringing the life of the Father, saves us. You see that we receive a new heart by the entering

into our lives of this new spirit, just as a new
love changes the heart. We are selfish; we care
for nobody; suddenly a new love comes into
our hearts; at once it possesses us and masters
us; we cannot get rid of it even if we would.
Like that is the love of Christ; coming to us as
an expulsive power; driving out selfishness and
sordidness and weakness and unbelief. So that
the salvation which Jesus Christ brings to us is
made real by the change which comes over our
lives. We are turned from doing wrong to doing
right, from the things which God hates to the
things which God loves.

And this is a permanent salvation—not a
transitory one; not depending upon our emotions. It is a permanent salvation because the
Lord Jesus Christ is an unchangeable Saviour.
"Jesus Christ the same yesterday, and to-day, and
forever." And when he says, " Come unto me,"
we know that he is " able to keep that which I
have committed unto him against that day."

The process, then, of becoming a Christian is
very simple. We discover our need and we ask
help. We hear a voice saying, " Come unto me
and live." We accept the invitation, and then we
begin to live, not for ourselves, but for " him who
died for us, and rose again." We ask, " Lord,
what wilt thou have me to do? "—that we may
do it. We ask, " Lord, what wouldst thou have

me to feel?"—that we may call upon our soul,
and all that is within us, to praise and mag-
nify his holy name. And when a man is willing
to do that he has met the Lord who has been
seeking him, and has found peace.

I have in my hand a letter written by one
who a short time ago was an unbeliever. He
says: "I do not doubt any longer. I accept the
simple fact that mankind was lost in sin; that I
have sinned; that I am to be saved by a redemption; that to accomplish a redemption there must
be a ransom; that this ransom must be Jesus
Christ, who is its center and head; that without
him there can be no redemption, and without
redemption the Christian religion is false." The
appeal of Jesus Christ to you, dear friends, is
along this line; simply that without argument
you recognize the fact that you are a sinner,
and that Jesus Christ has died for you, and that
he now offers himself as your ransom, and pleads
with you to let him lead you into life. And this
is the authentic record: "As many as received
him, to them gave he power to become the sons
of God."

XIV

AFTER DEATH—WHAT?

" 'Tis not the whole of life to live,
  Nor all of death to die."
                              JAMES MONTGOMERY.

" The death of the body is the separation of the soul from the body; but the death of the soul is the separation of the soul from God."   AUGUSTINE.

" I am most curious to get a glimpse of the next world. How will it all seem? Perfectly fair and perfectly natural, no doubt. We ought not to fear death; it is friendly."
                              GENERAL S. C. ARMSTRONG.

.

XIV

AFTER DEATH—WHAT?

THERE is a strange fascination about this question, After death—what? And it is not simply because death is to be the universal experience. Rather it is because there is something in every heart that tells us that the life which now is must stand in some essential relation to that which awaits us beyond the grave. For this reason man has always busied himself with questions concerning the life beyond. What are its characteristics; and is it a fact?

Before we can proceed to think of what we are to be we must know what we are. We look at a man—our friend—and we say, "What is he?" He is so much matter, so much intelligence, so much personal influence, so much political power, so much in productive force; and yet this is not the man. We get nearer to him and gaze upon his face, and we say, "This is my friend." He has an individuality which answers to something in ourselves. We separate him in thought from all others. We recognize that that separation is based upon something quite different from what is to be seen. We love him and cherish him and bind him to us "with hooks of steel," because of what we have discovered in him. That makes him the man we think him to be. When we have advanced as far as this in judging our friend we discover that in order to know him fully we must turn to ourselves. We are limited in our observation of him. We are conscious that back of all that any one can see or hear or discover in another there is the very self that lies within, and unrevealed.

So when we ask, "What is man?" we begin to inquire of our own hearts, and there we find an assemblage of feelings and impulses and affections and thoughts, all controlled and held together by what we call myself. Now we are getting nearer to the knowledge of what man is. He is myself—this person standing before you, being what he is. And as we proceed in our inquiries we recognize that what I am now I have always been, so long as I have been anything at all. Memory is the link that binds together the experiences which make up my life. I may forget many of the details of the life I have lived, but I recognize that through it all I have been essentially what I am now—myself.

But I am not simply an individual. A dog is an individual—that is, in those particulars in

which one dog differs from all other dogs; for
the individual dog acts under certain forces that
are in his nature, living, of course, below the plane
on which we live.   But I differ from all others
of my kind in a different way from that.

I have what we call a personality.   It is what
lifts man above all animals.   It is that in us which
can understand the past and gather unto itself all
the forces of the present, the person.

The question, then, is, What will death do for
this person?   No one comes back from beyond
death to tell us his experience, and continually we are reminded that because of this all our
thoughts about death must be guesses.   If they
are mere thoughts, opinions, inquiries, why concern ourselves about the matter?   Better attend
to the practical questions of daily life.   " Better
be a good man than a philosopher or a psycholo-
gist," some one has cynically said.   Yes; but our
being a good man, our being any kind of a man, will
be largely determined by the thoughts and conceptions we have not only of the present life, but
of the life that is to come.   We know that what
earnest men have done for us in the past by the
thoughts they have given us is still a potent force
in the life we are living.

And what is death?   We do not know what is
beyond, but we have a very graphic and definite
knowledge of what death is here.   That strange

hour has come which we all knew would come, and men say, "He is dying." He lies there on his bed. The forces of the body are ebbing. The blood is ceasing to course in the brain. The strong hand is palsied and nerveless. The eyes are closed, the sight is waning. The voices in the ear have ceased to be heard. The thoughts are far away. He can be summoned back only for a moment, as if already beyond our reach. He is no longer a part of the life which he has been living. Now he is dead.

We see all that the word means, and the question comes, Where has he gone? What has he become? What is the relation between death and this which we call life, with all its tragedy, with all its unrevealed history, with all its mysterious secrets? What is life, viewed from the point where he is now?

We will not be deceived by any pseudo-immortality, any mere suggestion of an immortality which a critical examination does not sustain.

There are those who affirm that immortality is everywhere; that matter has an eternal existence; matter so strange, so stable, yet always in flux; changing always, yet never ceasing to be; as matter we shall live forever. But that conception of immortality does not satisfy us.

Others maintain that force is immortal. Binding all these atoms together is the force of nature,

acting universally and never passing out of existence; man as a part of that energy will exist
forever; immortality is the discovery of that fact.
But this also does not satisfy.

Then there are those who say that life is like a
drama; that we each in turn appear on the stage,
act our little part, and then vanish, and the play
of life goes on forever, to be enacted by those
who shall follow us; that is the meaning of immortality. But we cannot accept that. No admitted
loss of the individual or person will serve to answer our question whether there is life beyond
death.

Some contend that immortality consists in the
living thought; that man is brought into existence, and molded by God as the universe is
molded, and that thoughts are eternal. But this
again does not satisfy, because then also our individuality vanishes.

Still others assert that we must be content
with finding immortality in moral force—the con-
tribution which each man is permitted to make
to the sum total of good in the world. We each
live our little day, and so life perpetuates itself
and influence passes on unbroken. To claim more
than that, it is said, is egotistical. The old figure
is of the drop of water falling into the ocean; not
lost, but simply gone back to its own; never to
be separated again, but simply having had the

experience of being for a brief moment withdrawn. But neither can we accept this for life and death.

The question before us, as thoughtful men, is, Shall I live again—being myself and not another? How shall we find our answer to this? We may approach it in two or three different ways. There is a very strong presumption that because God has made man he has made him for himself. If there is a God he is eternal; he has no limitations; and if he has made man—as he says he has—in his own image, to think his thoughts, the reason for man's existence that availed at the beginning will always maintain so long as God himself is. So there is this presumption, I say, that if we are the children of God we shall dwell with God forever.

But beyond this there is the striking fact that man has always recognized in himself a permanent tendency to believe in such immortality. It is the foundation-thought of all religions, the one from out of which all religions have sprung. Man is a worshiping creature. There has never been an age or condition in which he has not given evidence of this tendency of the heart to believe that we shall live after death. Do not think for a moment that I mean that this tendency should be accepted as proof of the fact. But it has been discovered as a scientific fact that

man has a strange tendency to believe certain
things which on other grounds may be proved
to be true; for example, that truth is better than
falsehood, that honor is better than injustice. So
this universal expectancy becomes a strong presumption that there is a corresponding fact.

There is a peculiar phrase in the Book of Ecclesiastes, which you may not have noticed, as it is
obscured in our English translation. It is in the
third chapter and the eleventh verse. The writer
says, " God has set [or hidden] eternity in the
heart of man." That is the discovery of a wise
man probing his own heart to see what curious
facts he could find there. And because God has
put that thought in our heart, as he has put the
eye in our head, there is a strong presumption
that it corresponds to some great external fact—
something that will be found a reality in the life
that lies beyond.

Another step in our thought is the plan of the
revelation by which God has been teaching men
through all the centuries, the process by which
man has ever been advancing to higher things.
This revelation brings proof of immortality as it
proceeds. In the beginning of the Old Testament little or nothing is said about it. We infer
it. There is something in the story of Abraham that makes us believe that he was not satisfied with the things which he saw. He left

everything that men value in life—home, friends, country—and went forth; the writer of the Hebrews says that he sought another, a better country, and that "he looked for a city . . . whose builder and maker is God." Abraham is always represented as a man strangely indifferent to the things about him. Jacob, with all his shrewdness and his firm hold upon the things of this world, never is settled; to the last he is a pilgrim moving on to those "things to come," concerning which his father had testified. So with Moses, who forsook the treasures of Egypt and the luxury of the king's palace, "choosing rather to suffer affliction with the people of God, than to enjoy the pleasures of sin for a season; . . . not fearing the wrath of the king: for he endured, as seeing him who is invisible"—and all because he stood in some definite relation to the Canaan that lies beyond the Jordan of death.

Take such a psalm as the seventy-third. There we have the struggle in every age, and in all men's hearts, over the mysteries of daily life. The wicked have all that heart can desire, and the righteous have plenty of trouble. The psalmist says he was "envious, when he saw the prosperity of the wicked." "They are not in trouble as other men; neither are they plagued like other men." "Until I went into the sanctuary of God; then understood I their end." Then

he hastens to say, " So foolish was I, and ignorant: I was as a beast before thee. Nevertheless
I am continually with thee: thou hast holden me
by my right hand. Thou shalt guide me with
thy counsel, and afterward receive me to glory.
Whom have I in heaven but thee? and there is
none upon earth that I desire besides thee. My
flesh and my heart faileth: but God is the
strength of my heart, and my portion forever."

Then there is the Book of Job: it is a drama
of immortality, offering immortality as a fact—the
key to all the trouble that now is. The prophets
also are spokesmen of the other world. They see
visions and dream dreams, and come with messages to their countrymen, because Jehovah, the
God of Abraham, of Isaac, and of Jacob, is not
the God of the dead, but of the living.

So, as the story of revelation advances, this
underlying thought—always assumed, always
taken for granted—becomes clearer and more
definite; always as the goal of life, always as the
ideal attainment, always as the supreme reward
for which God made his creatures. This in the
Old Testament.

When, at the opening of the New Testament,
we ask what the Jews believed, we find in their
hearts a deep-rooted consciousness that their God
lives beyond the veil; the winds are his messengers, and his voice like the sound of many

waters; his eyes are as a flame of fire.   Then
comes the supreme revelation of the Lord Jesus
Christ, who in one sentence says, " I am the
resurrection, and the life: he that believeth in
me, though he were dead, yet shall he live."
He brought life and immortality to light.

Now, when we add to this testimony of revelation the conviction of immortality which we find
in the heart of man, we come to our conclusion.
After death—what?   Life!   Before death the
sickness, before death the tragedy; after death
the solution of the tragedy, the light in which
there is no darkness at all, the opening of the
spiritual vision, the lifting of the veil, the revelation of the Father, whose face his children shall
henceforth behold.

What then?   We must seek in that end the
one explanation of what we call life.   How else
can we explain the pain, the disappointments, the
discipline, the labor, the daily duty of the present
life—the trials so incessant, the results so trivial,
the struggles so wearisome, the joys, at the best,
so transient?

Look at it in the individual case: a poor girl
dying in shame—drowning her shame in suicide
—and the author of her ruin walking in honor,
having all that heart could wish.   How is the
tragedy to be justified?   The prisoner executed
by mistake, lynched, perhaps, by a mob because

of some sudden and frenzied fear on the part of the community; and the community losing its fear, getting over its panic, and awakening to discover its mistake—when too late. How is the mistake to be corrected? The prisoner, perhaps, a man who had spent his life in toil and suffering for others; his wife and children now robbed of a husband and father, the home desolate, the family scattered; the possibilities of growth and blessing for them all gone. Where is the balance of blind justice? Such things are happening every day. In the conviction that beyond death is to be found life, with vast possibilities of redress, is the only answer.

The second thought is that all doubts as to the reality of a life beyond the grave arise from the consciousness of sin. You remember that beautiful description in Wordsworth's "Ode to Immortality":

> "Trailing clouds of glory do we come
> From God, who is our home.
> Heaven lies about us in our infancy."

Who doubts that the babe has come from God? Who can question that as it rests in its mother's arms it rests in the divine arms? God has made it for himself. That babe grows by and by to be a young man; and now the description changes:

" . . . The Youth
Who daily from the East
Must travel, still is nature's priest,
And by the vision splendid
Is on his way attended.
At length the man perceives it die away
And fade into the light of common day."

This is the story of our life. If we had kept pure it would not be so. The doubt of immortality is possible only as sin and selfishness and worldliness get the mastery over our hearts. If we should strive to live as God made us we should always carry about with us that consciousness of God which many of us have left behind. We know that we have lost the sense of gratitude and dependence which we once had. Otherwise the vision of infancy would have been permanently real; otherwise the man who longs for knowledge of that world which lies beyond would have had it revealed to him as it is often revealed to dying saints. It is not so with us because we have destroyed our power to see; it is given to the pure in heart to see God.

Therefore the duty of cultivating this thought of immortality—to " lay hold on eternal life," as the injunction of the Scripture is, and to measure all things about us in life in their effect upon our hearts in their relation to eternity. Do they drag us down to the level of earth? Or do they draw the veil aside and reveal that which is above our heads?

In the Homeric tale, you remember, Achilles, the invincible hero, said, "I would rather be a slave in the field for a poor man, than to be a king among the dead." To him the abode of the dead was the realm of unburied ghosts and the unrealities of existence. To the Christian the place of the dead is his Father's house; the end of weariness and the reward of toil; the city that came down from God out of heaven, adorned as a bride for her husband, which has no need of the sun, or of the moon, to shine in it, for the Lamb is the light thereof; where there is no death or sighing or pain or tears; where is the river of the water of life, and where his servants do serve him day and night in his temple. Blessed be God for the sure revelation of the life that is to come, and now is!

XV

SOME FEATURES OF IMMORTALITY

"Why, then, should witlesse man so much misweene
That nothing is but that which he hath seen?"

SPENSER, "Faerie Queene."

"We do not enter into a state of happiness merely from being buried. Many will seek happiness in the future life, and in the infinite series of future worlds, as much in vain as in the present life, if they think it can be found in anything but that which is now so near to them that it never can be brought nearer, viz., the Eternal."

SHEDD, "History of Doctrine," vol. ii., p. 423.

XV

SOME FEATURES OF IMMORTALITY

THE difference between a Christian and one who is not a believer in the Lord Jesus Christ is not simply in the fact that the one has a more definite hold on the life beyond the grave than the other, but also in the fact that his knowledge concerning things beyond the grave rests on what are to him matters of certainty. If, then, we turn aside from the declarations of the New Testament as to the other life, and occupy our thoughts with such suggestions as come to us out of our daily life, it is not because we are not satisfied with what the New Testament reveals, but simply because we desire to read what God has made more or less plain in his other book—the book of nature.

I think we may say that, in our last discussion approaching the thought in this way, we found abundant evidence to lead us to believe that death does not end all; that man is by nature immortal; and that the longings which come to us here are to find fulfilment hereafter.

But this simple fact can never satisfy us; for at once a multitude of questions arise in regard to the nature of that other life. We are convinced of an immortality of the conscious self. Now what are the leading features of that immortality —apart from rewards and punishments? What are to be what we may call its natural and inherent features?

One of them is that memory will certainly play a leading part in that future life. Memory seems essential to our identity on earth. Not that our continued existence, as being always the same person, is established or created by memory. As we look into our hearts and take cognizance of ourselves we find within a faculty which, not content with recording what we are now, continually runs back into the past, reviewing and estimating it. We may not remember what we did last year, or what we said—for memory plays us many tricks—but we do discover in our memories of the past that we were ourselves yesterday, and were equally so in the earliest recollections we have. It was myself who acted. It was myself who thought. It was myself who willed. It was myself who was responsible for what I did in this or that. In other words, memory brings to us evidence of the continued identity of self, and all this in the face of the fact that memory seems so uncertain and incomplete. We have lapses of memory, but when memory reasserts itself it bears testimony to the same truths to which it bore testimony before; and as we come to examine the place of memory in our lives, the wonder is not that we remember things, or that we remember things so minutely, but that we ever forget things; for memory is constantly surprising us with the fullness of the details that it carries with it; and from time to time peculiar experiences occur, as in the presence of death, when memory proves its power by flashing upon us all our past history in a moment. We may be sure, therefore, that as memory plays so important a part in our life on this side the grave, it will do the same on the other side.

We are aware, also, that this condition of things to which memory certifies has an effect in working out character quite independently of the outward circumstances of life. One lives in a palace, another in a hovel. One is learned in the knowledge of the world, another is ignorant. But we discover that the life of the ignorant man, or the life of the poorest and most circumscribed, may have in it elements of nobleness which are entirely independent of the external surroundings. So, then, memory, while it comes to us freighted with a diary of the past, also brings with it marvelous possibilities of attainment; and as the busy years go by, however they may serve to strip us of things which we treasure outside of ourselves, memory will ever carry on for us all that is best in thought, in attainment, in self-sacrifice, in achievement, no less than all that may have been worse. I think that this is one of the most patent and essential facts of that immortal life for which we all are destined.

And this leads to another question: Shall we recognize our friends in that other world? If our personal identity continues, then the identity of our friends will continue; and, startling as is the effect of death in its manifest power to strip man of all he has acquired in life, startling as is its power to level all to one common experience, so that it may literally be said of man, "Naked was he born, and naked shall he return to the earth," it nevertheless will remain a fact that the hand of death will be stopped at the point of its power to destroy our personal identity. We go down into death ourselves, and all that death can do is to strip us of our garments. If we are to live again we shall live as ourselves; and if we live ourselves, then our friends will live themselves.

Just now not infrequent reference is made to that passage in the New Testament which seems to antagonize this thought. I refer to Galatians iii. 28, where the Apostle says, "There is neither Jew nor Greek, there is neither bond nor free, there

is neither male nor female: for ye are all one in
Christ Jesus." And the inference is drawn that
by religion all distinctions of race or sex or condition are obliterated, and that therefore, in considering the structure of society or the relation
of man to man, it is right to ignore these relations. Such interpretation is an utter perversion
of the Scriptures. If you will take the trouble
to read the epistle you will see that the Apostle
is speaking of this single truth—that all men need
the gospel. Of that there is no question. To
the Jew and to the Greek, to the wise and to the
foolish, to the male and to the female, there is one
message, one redemption, one Saviour. All distinctions in this respect are banished forever. But
it was not at all in Paul's mind to ignore these
relations which God has established in nature
and life. These are permanent facts in human
history, because they are the products of the
history. And just as the Anglo-Saxon race has
its history, so that we cannot be other men than we
are, because of the blood that flows in our veins,
so other men are what they are—with their passions, with their limitations, with their marvelous
gifts, so different from ours, and yet so distinct and
powerful and useful in the world—because God
has "made of one blood all nations of men for
to dwell on all the face of the earth." The same
general conditions of oneness and of diversity are

true of all.   And while there is one Lord, one
faith, and one baptism, and all have the common
privileges of life, yet each comes as himself and
not as another, with his own history unalterable,
with his own individuality entering into and giving an account of what he is.   Now because of
this we find that the beauty of life and the power
of life are due to these differences.   In that other
life shall all the thought of God and the plan of
God be set aside and counted as if it were nothing?   Shall all that adorns this life be regarded
as forever banished from the life that is to come?

Paul, writing to the Thessalonians, comforts
them over their dead with the promise of the
Lord's coming again and bringing with him "ten
thousand of his saints," to meet those who sur-
vive till then on earth.   And John, in the Revelation, sees the New Jerusalem not only as a city,
that is, a place of elect companionships, but he
sees a great multitude out of every nation and
kindred and people and clime, recognizable, therefore, as retaining their own characteristics, each
one being himself and not some other.   What we
are here, because we are conscious persons, we
shall remain there—the man carrying with him
all that goes to make up his vigorous manhood,
and the woman all that constitutes her gracious
womanhood.   Let us not, then, in our concern
for the life that now is, and in our eagerness to

get support for schemes of social reform, pervert the Scriptures.

As we recognize ourselves, so shall we recognize our friends. Memory holds the strings of the heart forever. Dives remembers that he has five brethren, and pleads for them that they may not suffer the torment in which he finds himself. And when the veil is withdrawn on the Mount of Transfiguration, two men, Moses and Elias—not two visionary figures—come to minister to the Saviour, as the men who of old opened their hearts to God, and who lived near to God, while the world lay in darkness. Those two men, being themselves, come to talk with Jesus of his death which he is about to accomplish, which they beheld far off, and which they would now understand in the fullness of its meaning. Wherever you open the New Testament you will find this as the underlying and indisputable inference: the same individuality and the same recognitions exist in the other world that exist in this.

Now as to the question of the relation of the soul to the body. It is manifest that we are not to be disembodied spirits. We know that under the terms of man's material constitution the body is the soul's natural organ. We know the soul only as in the body. Its existence outside of the body and apart from the body is hard to

conceive. We know that a man in a certain
body here would become to us some one else if
he were out of that body or in a different body.
The body is not a machine on which the soul
can play as on a piano. It is not a casket in
which the soul is shut up to be kept from harm,
as a jewel in a case; and yet we often speak of the
body as " this poor, frail, worn-out body," from
which we would gladly escape. But what is this
body? It is so far my very self that separated
from it I could not understand myself and would
be some other than myself. As far as our experience goes, the soul is always in and of the
body.

The question how the soul came to be in the
body has never been answered. There are two
theories about it, the Traducian and the Creation.
According to the former the soul was born in the
same process by which the body was born. The
idea is old, and has been associated with many
great names. But there are manifest difficulties
regarding it—difficulties so great that it has never
gained a very firm hold on the world at large.

The other theory is that while the body is
produced as all animal life is, each separate soul
is a distinct creation; when the body is prepared
in the natural way then God bestows on it the
gift of a soul, as when God made Adam and
"breathed into his nostrils the breath of life; and

man became a living soul." There is a passage found in the twelfth chapter of Hebrews, at the ninth verse, which, if it be not decisive, as some would regard it, is suggestive. It reads: " Furthermore, we have had fathers of our flesh which corrected us, and we gave them reverence : shall we not much rather be in subjection unto the Father of spirits, and live?" It sets over against and in sharp contrast to the "fathers of our flesh " the " Father of spirits." The body is our earthly inheritance, given to us in the course of nature; but for each one the soul is in a special sense the divine gift, coming from the " Father of spirits," in whom " we live, and move, and have our being."

But be the theory what it may, the fact seems to be perfectly clear that the soul stands in some permanent relation to the body, which is essential to the soul's life. Paul dwells on this very fully in that wonderful fifteenth chapter of 1 Corinthians, emphasizing the fact, but not explaining the theory. He says: "As we have borne the image of the earthly we shall also bear the image of the heavenly ;" and then he promptly adds: " But this I say, brethren, that flesh and blood cannot inherit the kingdom of God ; neither doth corruption inherit incorruption. Behold, I show you a mystery ; We shall not all sleep, but we shall all be changed." That is the mystery: that this

earthly body, this piece of clay, is of the earth
and yet not of the earth; as flesh and blood it
does not remain, but in some strange change, as
not a terrestrial but a celestial body, it is still to
inherit the kingdom of God.

Were we asked, " How is it possible that there
can be any other conception of the body than
the material?" we answer that it all turns on
our idea of the nature of matter. We talk very
learnedly of matter. We separate matter from
spirit, and we say that matter is " impenetrable,"
" indestructible," " indivisible," and many other
things; but what do we know about matter?
Two corks, dropped into the water, slowly move
toward each other; what causes them to do
so? We call it attraction. What does that
mean? What quality has matter, that force can
act from one body to another through space?
We are told that each atom of matter is composed of molecules that are in incessant motion,
and the phenomena of matter are due to their
impact. What, then, is matter? Who can tell?
The mathematician talks to us about the fourth
dimension of space. We do not understand what
that can mean. All goes to show that this earth,
this footstool of God upon which we live, is a
most mysterious thing. We know really nothing
about it. How, then, shall " this mortal put on
immortality," and how shall "this corruptible put

on incorruption "?   Who can answer?   "Behold,
I show you a mystery ; We shall all be changed."
But we shall still be ourselves.

What, then, is to follow death?   There certainly will be no suspension of existence.   As
we have no evidence of annihilation—and we
should need most conclusive evidence to believe
it—so we have no evidence of a conditional immortality.   The presumption is strong against
both, and the testimony of Scripture seems clear.
These theories have gained credence chiefly as
convenient doctrines for escaping the force of the
many and plain scriptural declarations of a coming
judgment and eternal punishment.

Nor will there be any intermediate state of un-
consciousness or of unrealized hope. The Saviour's
promise, " To-day shalt thou be with me in paradise," and the Apostle's assurance of being "ever
with the Lord," would seem to shut out such uncertainty.   The testimony of the Scripture is that
in death we pass through the veil to the immediate life beyond, for which every Christian heart
has yearned—longing to be unclothed that we
may be clothed upon—where for the believer all
life's pains and tears shall be left forever behind,
and where " death is swallowed up in victory."

We are all destined to a permanent existence,
carrying with us this very body in which we
have lived and loved below.   And there " every

one of us shall give account of himself to God." If this is true, then to live here is to be on trial for the life beyond. It is to be in a state of preparation for that immortality which is daily opening before us. Earth becomes not the portal to that life, but a part of it. In that sense life is a time of probation. "To-day, if ye will hear his voice, harden not your hearts." It is possible for us so to open our hearts, so to surrender ourselves to the divine arms, that life yonder shall come to us as a blessing and not as a dread; that continued existence shall be not a regret and not a pain, but the great reward. "My flesh and my heart faileth," said the psalmist; and our hearts and flesh fail with the continued burdens and cares and disappointments of life; but as he added, so may we add, "God is the strength of my heart, and my portion forever."

"Thou hast made me for thyself, O God, and my heart cannot rest until it findeth itself in thee." That is the testimony of every truth-telling heart, bearing witness to itself and its destiny.

XVI

PAUL'S IDEA OF HEAVEN

"No; I do not want to see the heavens open like Stephen, unless He choose to open them. No; I do not ask to see the New Jerusalem like John, unless He think this best. Gethsemane seen by faith is to me the gate of heaven, and Calvary sparkles and shines to me, the sinner, with brighter rubies than the city not made with hands; it shines with the rubies of His dying love. I have not seen them with these eyes, but He who died for me sent me word concerning them, and I gratefully believe."

REV. W. G. SCHAUFFLER, D.D.,
Sermon in Constantinople.

XVI

PAUL'S IDEA OF HEAVEN

WE have devoted two discussions to the consideration of the question of a continued existence
after death. We come now to what the Bible has
to say about the nature of life beyond the grave,
and more particularly to Paul's idea of heaven.

The evidence that God's hand was from the
beginning upon the children of Israel is found in
the fact that after two hundred and possibly four
hundred years of civilized life in Egypt they came
up out of Egypt entirely free from the supersti-
tions of Egypt in regard to the other world. Of
all the nations of antiquity the Egyptians believed
that the things that are seen are the unreal
things. This life to them was not only wrapped
about with immortality, but was filled with the
consciousness of the presence of unseen beings.
Their vast monuments are all associated with the
dead—those who were either dead when the
monuments were erected, or were preparing to
die. The mummy was made for the chief pur-

pose of preserving the soul, which needed to have a local habitation; and all the circumstances attendant upon their burial of the dead and their ritual of worship are emblematical of that truth. The remarkable fact is that the Hebrews could be so long in contact with all this and come forth untouched by it.

So one evidence of the presence of God in the Christian church, as furnishing a positive revelation of God to his people, is found in the fact that the church has kept itself so free from the opinions of men. There has always been an abundance of people ready to tell us what heaven is; sometimes in words so excited as to be almost incoherent; always ending with, "It may be so;" and in no case furnishing a basis for an intelligent faith. Now I say that the Christian church has, by the grace of God, been kept free from ever making much of this idea of the other life, and has been able to hold itself content with what God has chosen to reveal in his Word. Therefore it is with confidence and with a real and grateful sense of rest that when a question so interesting as this—one that appeals to every heart—comes up we turn to the New Testament and ask what the Lord himself has to say of that blessed life where we are to be "hid with Christ in God."

You may remember that the Second Epistle of Paul to Timothy is apparently the last writing of that great apostle. He is in prison at Rome. His life has been most eventful, and from an earthly standpoint a failure. But he knows whom he has believed, and is persuaded that God is able to keep that which he has committed to him against that day. In his farewell to his beloved Timothy he uses these somewhat notable words: "Henceforth," he says, "there is laid up for me a crown of righteousness, which the Lord, the righteous judge, shall give me at that day: and not to me only, but unto all them also that love his appearing." He is writing, as I have intimated, his last words. About him are all the signs of his failure and the instruments of pain. He is in fetters in a cell. He says, "I am already being offered;" using a word that is associated with sacrifice—"I am being poured out," as oil or wine is poured out. "The time of my departure is at hand": he adopts a nautical term—not as a sailor going out of a harbor upon an unknown ocean, but with a chart and compass, knowing from whence he has come and whither he is going, he is about to put to sea. The walls of the prison vanish, and he sees himself once more in the arena, as he says, "I have fought "— not *a* good fight, but—"I have fought *the* good fight."

Then he sees the race-course stretching out before him, and the thought of the prizes of the

Olympic contests comes to his mind: "I have run the race, the goal is within my reach;" but feeling the insufficiency of the metaphor, conscious that it is no earthly contest in which he is engaged, he exclaims, "I have finished my course, I have kept the faith: henceforth [now that all is done] there is laid up for me a crown of righteousness, which the Lord, the righteous judge, shall give me at that day: and not to me only, but unto all them also that love his appearing," and for whom he had labored and prayed and sacrificed, and who were waiting for the manifestation that is to come.

Here we have the Apostle's idea of heaven. Back of it in the New Testament there lies very little. The Saviour had come and made his revelation of God, and had entered into his reward; and how little he had said of that future! "If I go and prepare a place for you, I will come again, and receive you unto myself; that where I am, there ye may be also. "That was enough. He was speaking to men and women who had found their chief delight in being with him, and the sum of whose sorrow was to be separated from him even for the brief hours of the crucifixion.

"In that day ye shall ask me nothing," he says. After the resurrection they pressed no question upon him concerning that life from the portal of which he was talking to them. It was enough for them to know that heaven is to be where he is. They were to be with him and be like him, and that was sufficient. But now the years have gone by, and they have been called upon to bury their dead; the apostles, the elders in the churches, the wives, the fathers, the little children, had been one by one laid in their graves; and we see in the catacombs pictured testimony to the faith they had in the reality of the life into which they had gone: the shepherd with his flock, the ship in full sail, the winged dove. It is not strange that Paul's first letter to the Thessalonians—the first, indeed, of all he wrote—should have been called forth by questions concerning their dead —"Where are they, what are they doing, and when shall we see them again?" And you remember that Paul comforts them by such words as "I would not have you to be ignorant, brethren, concerning them which are asleep, that ye sorrow not, even as others which have no hope," etc.

I speak of this simply to show you that these questions were uppermost in the minds of those early Christians, even as hearts are constantly torn by them. And now Paul has the future in mind, and his last words are like his first—words of revelation. He says, "What I have, I have received from God;" and he goes on to show that God has condescended to give him a revelation of himself and of all that he needs to know of that world which lies beyond. He is in no uncertainty and he has no further care.

What, then, do his words declare? What is the idea of heaven which Paul possessed?

In the Greek contests the victor ran or struggled for a definite prize. It was the one particular prize of that contest in his eyes. It was no chance. And Paul now says, as the Greek shows, "I have won the prize." Heaven is to be to me the place of my desire, the attainment of my hopes, the fulfilment of all my longings. It is to be home, the place I have struggled for, and which I have won. It is to be the crown of my rejoicing.

"Henceforth there is laid up for me the crown of righteousness"—the sum of all that he had hoped for. That is a strange word—"the crown of *righteousness*"—a word seemingly entirely out of place; one we would not have anticipated in this connection. To the Jews " righteousness " was something external and visible; something that could be attained by ritual and service. But Paul was no longer a Jew. The figures of the Old Testament had, for him, been broken into pieces, and recreated and filled with special truth such as the Old Testament had not contained; so that he says that righteousness is no longer the possession of the law. It is that which he had come to know in the life and teaching of the

Lord Jesus Christ, his Saviour, his Friend; and now, having spent the years of his service under the dominion of Christ, having schooled himself to have ambitions, desires, and longings all within the conception of what had come to him through Christ, he finds himself so saturated, so steeped, we might say, in Christ that he longs to depart and be with him.

In the Old Testament the holy meant to the Jew that which God had chosen—the ark, the altar, the tabernacle, the day, the place, the person—whatever was characterized as holy was so not because of any quality in itself, nor because of anything that man had done in connection with it, but because God had chosen it, for reasons of his own. Then the thought advanced from that to the idea that what God had chosen must be kept pure and clean. Therefore the ark was to be undefiled by human touch, and the holy of holies unapproached; the priests were to wear holy garments; the camp was kept sedulously clean; and the life of a man chosen by God must be a cleanly life, because God's choice rested upon him. From that the step was short to a third consideration: whatever God had chosen must be set apart from all other uses; the Sabbath and the temple and the altar belonged to God, and were not to be desecrated. These thoughts underlay the Jewish conception of holiness. But now it had been lost sight of, and the Jew had come to think that men can make themselves holy; that a man can set himself apart; that he can make himself worthy to be chosen of God, and therefore that God must choose him. Paul takes this meaning of the word and shows the weakness of it. The burden of his preaching has been that all men are sinners: "There is none righteous, no, not one." Righteousness is only by the gift and calling of God, and it is in Jesus Christ. Christians are to live for this crown of righteousness to which they have been called of God, and live as men set apart—righteous, holy —because accepted of God. So that Paul's idea of heaven is the "fulfilment of righteousness." It is to be that place in which God's choice of him will be manifest, and in which the surrender of his life to God shall be finally accomplished; he is no more to be dragged down to earth, but to live in that fellowship with God for which, like a prince or a king, he was born.

This conception in Paul's mind involves two distinct things. In the first place, heaven is a place of deliverance from sin. No man knew better what sin is than Paul. That he might be delivered from sin had been the prayer of his life. He had fought it continually; he bore the signs of the "body of death" about with him.

Long ago he had learned that " the sting of death is sin." Now the final struggle is the signal of deliverance. The angel of death comes bringing the palm-branch and the crown. He will lay his finger upon that bowed and battered frame, and in an instant the fetters will be broken, the grasp of the tempter will relax, and the soul, purified of every spot and scar of the struggle in which it has been so long engaged, will leap up into the celestial radiance and find itself fitted to share the life of those who dwell with God.

He knew that heaven could not consist of a mere outward vision. He had seen his Lord. He had opened his heart that it might be " the temple of the Holy Ghost "; and now, looking into his heart—still scarred with the guilt of sin, so that he should speak of himself as the chief of sinners—he says, " Henceforth there is laid up for me a crown of righteousness, which the Lord, the righteous judge, shall give me at that day."

We have only to look into our own hearts to know what this means. What will it avail, dear friends, to you or to me to have " a new heaven " or " a new earth," unless you and I there shall find ourselves freed from the power of temptation? Of what use are palm-branches and psalms of praise put into the hands and on the lips of men and women who still feel themselves weak before their own passions, or subject to the possibility of falling under some sudden temptation, or carrying in their hearts the terrible secrets of a misspent life? It is because heaven will bring deliverance that, when weary of the struggle, we long for it. It is because there he will be " washed white in the blood of the Lamb," and forever beyond the contact of evil, that the believer desires to depart and be with Christ.

Said the saintly Anselm, " If I were called to choose between the terrors of hell and the pains of sin I would rather be in hell and be innocent than in heaven and carry in my heart the consciousness of my own guilt." Of course he knew the impossibility of such a thing. But the thought is that there can be no heaven to a man who is still under the burden of his sins. To Paul, more than all else was the thought of the blotting out of his sin and its being remembered no more.

But I said heaven had to Paul a twofold aspect. Deliverance from sin was to the Apostle only the negative side of the truth. To him heaven was also to be a place of the sudden revelation of the glories of righteousness. In an instant the trial will be over, the temptation ended, the crown awarded. " The babe, all sense, that creeps upon the lap of earth," will become, to use the language of another, " the being, all seraph, that basks in the open splendors of the living God."

How little we know of righteousness now!
How little we know of the glories of a holy
character! How little we can see of the meaning of the simple word of the Saviour, "The
pure in heart shall see God"! Where in all the
realms of earth is there a heart pure enough for
that? And now Paul had before him the conception of a life in which the unrevealed glories
of the righteous God should dawn upon his soul.

What is to be the nature of that revelation?
It is to be a revelation of knowledge. The re-
deemed soul is to find itself, as it were, at the
center of all God's thought and all God's doing.
As at the center of a circle all is seen harmoni-
ous, while from any other point it is unbalanced
and irregular, so from that standpoint, hid with
Christ in God, the vast circumference of all God's
wonderful ways will be understood. "The weary
weight of all this unintelligible world" will roll
away before the vision of truth. Pain—that
great mystery in all our lives—will then be recognized as God's blessed minister of peace and
of preparation; and the sorrows in which we find
it so hard to see God's hand we shall then discover to be the crowning acts of his tenderness,
his wisdom, and his love. We shall then see
God not only as he is, but as he has been in all
his dealings with us. We shall know what that
word "God is love" means; and as we look back

upon our past lives, with their weaknesses and failures and half-hearted submission to God's providences, we shall find that God's love has been with us from the beginning.

Now what shall be the occupations of such a heaven? Why need we ask? Surely they will be no mere idle contemplation, no mere waving of palm-branches and singing of psalms; for all the labor of life has been discipline, and all this long striving after knowledge so hard to get, and so hard to make use of when once acquired, will be but the beginning of that life where we shall think God's thoughts and find delight in doing God's will. What room for delightful and ceaseless employment does this suggest, in a world where there is neither weariness nor pain!

All this simply sets forth this truth that heaven begins in the heart. It consists not in externals, but in the growth of that which is within. As the flower is the putting forth of the life that was in the seed, so heaven is the flowering forth of that truth and life of God which has been hidden in our hearts here on earth. The rewards of heaven are to be the development of what is within us, rather than the addition of something from without. A perfect holiness, a crown of righteousness! Why need we seek to add more to our knowledge of heaven than this? If this does not appeal to us, can it be that we are not

ready for heaven; that we are not fitting ourselves for that life in which the pure are not only
to see God, but are to be with God? Can it be
that any of us are praying, as young Augustine
did, " O Lord, make me pure, but not yet "?

The mystery is how it is possible that hearts
like yours and mine, as we know ourselves, shall
ever be so changed; shall ever be so freed, not
only from their past sins, but from their present;
from what you and I are to-day and every day
—so freed from all this that we shall be fitted for
the presence of the holy God. And yet that is
God's sure word of promise. " They that have
washed their robes," who have been pardoned
and cleansed in the blood of Jesus Christ, who
have done as Paul did—filled their lives with
Christ—" shall enter in through the gates into
the city." For that city is their home; and the
Lord has come to take them one by one—you
and me and all who love him—unto himself, that
where he is, there we may be also.

XVII

JOHN'S IDEA OF HEAVEN

" Ye stars are but the shining dust
    Of my divine abode;
The pavement of the heavenly court
    Where I shall reign with God."

PHILIP DODDRIDGE.

XVII

JOHN'S IDEA OF HEAVEN

I THINK that every one recognizes the fitness of rendering the descriptions which John gives in the Apocalypse of the Holy City, the New Jerusalem, in music; for these descriptions are poetic images, and we have no language or form of expression so fit to convey the thought as that available in music. These images were more familiar to the Jewish mind than they are to us. The writings of the prophets are full of them.

Many years ago I saw in the Pitti Palace in Florence a famous painting by Raphael of Ezekiel's vision of the cherubim, and the living creature within the wheels. Many of you have seen it. There were the visible figures; but you undoubtedly turned away from the picture, as I did, unsatisfied, and with the deepening conviction in your heart that there was given to the prophet an ability to depict the scene which was not given to the painter. So it was with John in his description of his wonderful vision. He says:

"He carried me away in the spirit to a great and high mountain, and showed me that great city, the holy Jerusalem, descending out of heaven from God, having the glory of God: and her light was like unto a stone most precious, even like a jasper stone, clear as crystal." Then he goes on to describe the walls and the gates of the city as made of precious stones and pearls; and lest we should think that he was describing earthly jewels, he at once adds, "And the city had no need of the sun, neither of the moon, to shine in it: for the glory of God did lighten it, and the Lamb is the light thereof;" and then in the most graphic language he tells us that "the nations of them which are saved shall walk in the light of it: and the kings of the earth do bring their glory and honor into it. And the gates of it shall not be shut at all by day: for there shall be no night there."

To understand this Book of Revelation it is necessary to grasp the purpose of it; and the apostle is very careful that he should not be misunderstood in this. The aim of the book is not to describe heaven, but to counsel and strengthen and admonish the children of God. They were few in number, surrounded by the vast world of heathenism, uncertain themselves of the Christian life into which they were called, and already in sharp controversy among themselves. The aged apostle receives from the loving-kindness of the Master this vision of the heavenly life, that by it he may interpret to these poor, troubled Christians the joys that are in store for those who, having overcome, shall enter into their reward. He declares it at the very opening of the book, in his message to the seven churches. Violent death stared them in the face; he tells them of the tree of life. Some had given up what worldly wealth they had, and social position; he sets before them citizenship in the New Jerusalem. Some were outcasts, hiding in caves and mountains; he describes the paradise of God, with its streets of gold and gates of pearl. Some were forsaken by their friends; he tells them of the hidden manna and the white stone with the new name written on it. They were to endure hunger and cold and nakedness; he tells them of the life where the Good Shepherd gathers the lambs in his arms and leads his flock beside the still waters. Some were already discouraged; he tells them of the crowns of glory which await those who hold fast their faith unto the end. In other words, all his thought is to lead them to see the blessings that shall come to them in the final triumph of the Lord whom they serve. He seeks to impress them with the thought that Jesus was no mere Jewish Messiah, living his brief earthly life and going down into a grave of obloquy with an unfinished and hope-less work lying about him. He has come from the throne of the Father, where the apostle is permitted to see him, with the flaming sword in his hand, and surrounded by the great multitude whom no man can number.

This is something of the vision; and though its metaphors are strange to us, and its imagery unusual, yet there are certain definite truths which I am sure, dear friends, we shall be able to grasp and carry away with us for our daily lives.

The first of these truths is this: that all this imagery is intended to represent a glorious ex-istence which our minds in their present earthly condition are not adequate fully to comprehend. It is to be a real existence, but indescribable. Many have tried to describe it. Picture to your-self the heavens thickly studded with stars, the horizon with its zenith, the hills clad with ver-dure, the valleys decked with bloom of flowers and musical with the ripple of streams; try to imagine all this, and see how it fails to fit into the statement, " The city had no need of the sun, neither of the moon, to shine in it: for the glory of God did lighten it, and the Lamb is the light thereof." You are not one step nearer an idea of heaven. A vision was given to the prophet of an existence so beautiful that even the radi-ant light of the sun is dull and commonplace in comparison. It suggests that which does not belong to this earth; it is to be a spiritual existence. Then we ask, "What is a spiritual existence?" and we find that we do not know. He speaks of "a new heaven" and "a new earth" and "a new creation" coming down from God to men. We do not know how the visible universe shall end its relations to ourselves, and we certainly do not know what shall follow after it. "We shall be changed;" that, in Paul's phrase, is the great mystery. That it covers a blessed truth is manifest whenever we open this Book of Revelation, bringing, as it does, the conception of a life so full, so satisfying, so enduring, that all that lies behind us shall be forgotten.

Again, we observe that, according to John, the glory of heaven centers in none of these things which he tries so hard to describe; the glory of heaven is found in the presence of God. "And I heard a great voice out of heaven saying [just when his hearers are ready for the description of the New Jerusalem], Behold, the tabernacle of God is with men, and he will dwell with them, and they shall be his people, and God himself shall be with them, and be their God." Then when he proceeds to describe the New Jerusalem he says, "And I saw no temple therein." The most beautiful, the most imposing structure in any ancient city was the temple; and it was

therefore the temple up to which all his preliminary descriptions should have led—the gates and
walls are but incidents as he comes nearer to
the temple; and when all are ready to have him
speak of that crowning glory of the city, he
stops. " And I saw no temple therein: for the
Lord God Almighty and the Lamb are the temple of it." He fixes our thought upon this great
truth that the life and the joy and the service of
all who enter into the life beyond are to be found
in the presence with them of God.

Now the Old Testament had taught this from
the beginning. There was that man to whom
God had revealed himself, " and he was not; for
God took him." There was that other, led up
into the mountain, while God covered him with
his hand and caused all his goodness to pass before him, and showed him, as he said, " only his
hinder parts," for " no man can see his face and
live "; and when Moses came down from the
mountain his face shone so that the people were
afraid, and he had to put a veil over his face.
Then there was the prophet by the ancient waters
of Babylon, who had that wonderful vision of
things so hard to understand; then the vision on
the Mount of Transfiguration; and now this to
John, where the horizon lifts and the clouds are
changed into the walls and palaces of the heavenly
city, and the light that never was on land or sea

shone down upon him, and he is wrapped about with the surpassing glory of the divine presence.

This is John's conception of the heavenly city, very real and very tangible, as you see; for he immediately hastens to say, "And God himself shall be with them, and be their God. And God shall wipe away all tears from their eyes; and there shall be no more death, neither sorrow, nor crying, neither shall there be any more pain: for the former things are passed away."

Now, if we cannot tell our children that they shall have all the pleasures which have been so real and so precious to them on earth, we can tell them of the Good Shepherd who calls his sheep by name, and his sheep shall know his voice, and he shall lead them forth, and they shall follow him. And if we do not know where our friends are who have already passed through the dark waters and have vanished from our sight, and what are their occupations and what is their bodily form, we can still say, "Thou hast taken them to thyself. Thou hast hidden them in thy pavilion from the strife of tongues." And he that dwelleth in the secret place of the Most High shall forever abide under the shadow of the Almighty. They have all that heart could wish, for their life centers in him who is the center of the heavenly home.

One thing more. John makes it very plain

that all these glories of heaven which so filled and satisfied his heart depend upon personal purity. He hastens to say, "And there shall in no wise enter into it anything that defileth, neither whatsoever worketh abomination, or maketh a lie." Now we understand why he said at the beginning of the chapter, "There was no more sea." From the earthly standpoint, if the sea vanishes there will be no more earth. "But the wicked are like the troubled sea." The sea, which no man can master, and whose depths none can fathom, shall give up its dead; they shall come trooping forth obedient to the same voice that said, "Peace, be still."

How wonderful is the unity of the Bible! Last Sabbath evening we dwelt upon Paul's declaration, "Henceforth there is laid up for me a crown of righteousness, which the Lord, the righteous judge, shall give me at that day: and not to me only, but unto all them also that love his appearing." Then Peter tells us that we are to "look for new heavens and a new earth, wherein dwelleth righteousness"; and now John, having this vision of heaven, describes it, if not in the same words, at least with the same thought, as the Saviour had when he said, "Blessed are the pure in heart: for they shall see God." John's idea of heaven, Peter's idea of heaven, Paul's idea of heaven, no matter along what line they traveled, all come back to the same truth that only those whose hearts have been washed white and made clean in the blood of the Lamb shall enter in through the gates into the city; because, being made pure in heart, they shall see his face and be like him.

As we close two questions arise. First, Why is it that the Bible does not describe heaven to us more minutely, and make the joys of heaven more definite? The answer is not far to seek. Definite rewards enfeeble virtue and tend to destroy character; and this is at once the difference between the religion of Jesus Christ and all other religions. The Indian looks for the happy hunting-grounds of his fathers. To the Turk, with his Koran, heaven is a place of sensuous enjoyments. To the old Greeks their heroes became their gods to be worshiped. But to the Christian heaven is a place where are realized the joys of the purified heart. It is to be life in the soul and not in the senses. It is to be the consummation of all that men have striven for in their best estate, in their most exalted hours, when they have been lifted most above the power of temptation.

We like to recall and associate with our friends, when they have passed beyond the veil, their various occupations in life. We think of the kindly neighbor and his many acts of thoughtful-

ness; of the teacher in his school; of the pastor
in his pulpit and among his people; but we are
aware that these associations fall short of com-
pleting the conception of our friend's character.
He has entered into that which we do not know.
He must be engaged in occupations larger than
any which occupied him here.   There are doubtless other occupations in heaven than singing
hymns.   Shall we wonder what the Christian is
doing because the Bible speaks only of these?
What is the Christian's life but one long psalm
of praise, on the street, in the workshop, in the
school, in the home, wherever he is?   I might
easily

> " Unleash my fancy, if you wish,
> And hunt for phantoms ; shoot an airy guess,
> And bring down airy likelihood,"

with regard to the service and the joys of that
other life ; but what wiser would we be?   It is
enough for us to know that " it is far better to
depart, and be with Christ."   Therefore the blessed
mystery which inwraps our friends who " are not;
for God has taken them."

And the other question is, What is there of
practical value to be gained from all this?   It
gives us the conception of a heaven which starts
with this earthly life.   We are to find our reward there for all that we have done for God
here.   No thought, no act, of service, no tempta-

tion resisted, no Christian effort put forth, nothing done for Christ and in the consciousness of his call to follow him, but shall find its place there, as it has found already its place here in fitting us for that life of which the very last words of the apostle were, " His servants do serve him." As on earth we get our best service from chosen men, so God has taught us that he works by the hand of fit men; therefore by so much as we have fitted ourselves for work here, shall we be fitted to do his bidding there.

And as to the rewards and joys of that life— all are to be measured by our capacity to receive them. So we are all of us making our own heaven every day. If the presence of Christ is precious to us here, it will be more precious there. If the thought of the divine righteousness is helpful to us here, it will be the sustaining thought there. Pain and sorrow and sickness, when they come to us, are always accompanied with sharp stings, because they are always associated with our mistakes or our misdoings. What a marvelous meaning there is in John's description of that other life! " There shall be no more death, neither sorrow, nor crying, neither shall there be any more pain." It is proof that all sin shall be blotted out; buried in the depths of the sea; remembered no more. All this goes to show that something more than death is necessary to prepare us for heaven. Merely shuffling off this mortal coil will have small part in fitting any man or woman for the fellowship of the home above. What is to be said, then, of men and women who have no larger conception of the meaning of life than the pursuits and pleasures of the passing hour, while they indulge the foolish hope that the dropping of this mortal body is going to make real the joys and opportunities of heaven, and that losing the burden of the corruptible is going to secure to them the pleasures and triumphs of the incorruptible? It is because we are Christ's that we shall live. It is in him that we are to see the face of the Father, and by walking in his footsteps we are to find our way into the celestial city. Think of those who, at last, after long and weary wanderings, because they are Christ's and Christ is theirs, are to be blessed with a " sudden happiness beyond all hope " !

XVIII

THE JUDGMENT

"Nihil amplius quærendum est quam quod tradere Christi consilium fuit."   CALVIN, on Matthew xx. 1–16.

"A remark which I am convinced is true, namely, that the dread book of account which the Scriptures speak of is, in fact, the mind itself of each individual. Of this, at least, I feel assured—that there is no such thing as forgetting possible to the mind."   DE QUINCEY, "Opium-eater," p. 112.

XVIII

THE JUDGMENT

A VERY few words will suffice upon the theme before us. We are but little concerned about what man's opinion may be as to the judgment; but we all want to know what are God's statements in regard to it. We have seen in previous discussions how large is God's purpose of blessing for his children in the life beyond the grave, and how that purpose centers about God himself, the revelation of his character, and the unfolding of his plans from the creation onward. The glory of God no less than the righteousness of God is to be revealed in the final judgment. It is to be the day in which God shall set the seal on all that he has done.

There are many verses of Scripture that refer to the judgment; but one or two will suffice as well as a dozen, if we can understand exactly what their teaching is. One of the simplest statements of the Scriptures in regard to the judgment is in the Epistle to the Hebrews, at the twenty-seventh verse of the ninth chapter: " It is appointed unto men once to die, but after this the judgment." That little word "once" is more significant in the original than it is in our common version. It is " once for all." " It is appointed unto men once for all to die ;" an event which never can be repeated, and which carries in itself all possible consequences.

We all feel the significance of an event which happens but once. As a matter of historic fact, Julius Cæsar, when proconsul of Gaul, crossed the little bridge of the Rubicon, which was forbidden to him by law, with head erect, and eager hope. His eye was fixed on Ariminum, the first rendezvous of his troops on the soil of Rome. He was too used to victory to be careful now of consequences. But as men have read the history they have put words upon his lips: " The enemy awaits me, the opportunity invites, the die is cast." Instinctively we feel that the stoutest heart must tremble before any irrevocable step, because once taken it is taken for all time, and a man's destiny, if not the destiny of a nation, is settled.

Schiller's magnificent drama of " Wallenstein " turns on such a moment. At its opening the great duke stands studying the horoscope in regard to the hour from whose decision he knows there is no turning back. Shall he obey the emperor and resign his command, or shall he refuse and revolt? The drama thrills with the fatal indecision. At last the step is taken and he hastens to his tragic end.

You remember how Queen Elizabeth sat trembling, pen in hand, with the warrant for Mary Stuart's execution before her; and how, having signed it, she threw the pen on the floor in the vain attempt to escape the consequences.

Put yourself in one of these critical hours. Let this once-for-all event be not connected with anything we have seen or done, but the end of a life, the hour which, as we are taught by the Scripture, is destined to trammel up in itself the consequences of all the hours of the life we have been living—how significant it becomes! For death closes the past. However carelessly we have lived, or however wisely; however numerous our years, however empty or full, the past ends all.

And not only that; death opens for us once for all the future. And this is to be no less significant than the other. In daily life events constantly hurry us to consequences which we cannot comprehend. We are like travelers who are surprised with the familiar appearance of some foreign city. We look about astonished. We have heard of these strange sights, we have believed in them, or at least we thought we did. We almost fancy now that we have been here before; these stores and wharves, that public square

and monument, those faces and costumes—surely
we have seen them before. But no; before we
had only read of them or heard of them; now
we see them for ourselves. Before we only had
a faint idea of them; now comes the reality.
Quickly the mind adjusts itself to these scenes,
and then follows a strange sense of loneliness.
A new life, with altogether new experiences, has
opened to us.

How significant, then, when, having crossed,
not the untried ocean, but the ocean of death,
going out of this life as we all must go, we find
ourselves in the realities of the other world!
The word of the Scripture is, then, our tran-
scending thought: " It is appointed unto men
once to die "—that unknown experience, closing
the past, and bringing to light the things of the
future, is appointed once for all.

Then it is appointed once for all " unto men."
We are entirely familiar with the thought of
death as coming to some one else. It is a
strange experience only as it comes to ourselves
—to you and me. We find it hard even in our
most serious and thoughtful moments to understand what that experience will be. A crowd
gathers about the door, and the inquiry is raised,
" Who is it? " " Mr. A." " What! my friend? "
" Yes."   " Impossible; he was with us but a few
days ago in church, or at my house. It seems

but an hour since I was talking with him on the street; and now he is dead!"

It is appointed unto men, without exception, to die; and how soon every one of us shall know the reality! In fifty years who of us will not have experienced it? A hundred years and not one of us will be left. And after this universal experience comes the judgment.

It does not say immediately after, or how long after. That is unimportant. The significant part is that death and the judgment stand so related to each other. At once all questions as to an intermediate state, or as to a second and a new probation, settle themselves. All are definitely answered by the single statement "once for all," and after that "the judgment." All that is significant that can come to us gathers about those two events; the one of which is wrapped up in the other. As we have lived we meet death— every one of us; and as we meet death we meet the judgment.

What, then, is the event which is so interlinked with the universal experience of mankind? Here let us turn to another text, the twentieth chapter of Revelation, and the twelfth verse: "And I saw the dead, small and great, stand before God; and the books were opened: and another book was opened, which is the book of life: and the dead were judged out of those things which were written in the books, according to their works." You see how closely the statement links itself to the previous one, simply enlarging it—the "small and great," all who have passed through the common experience of death, are "judged out of the things written in the books."

We have previously considered how important a part memory plays in life. Memory does not constitute the identity of character, but it bears testimony to it. We remember what we did a year ago or ten years ago; whether or not we remember the details of the experience, we remember this fact that he who did the deed or saw the scene is this person who now remembers it. And thus the effect of memory is to bear testimony to the fact that we are ourselves. As long as we have lived we have been ourselves, and as long as we continue to live we shall remain ourselves. And the mystery of life is not that we remember the past, but that, the mind being what it is, we ever seem to forget it.

Now, in the light of this fact, comes the word of the Scripture, "The dead were judged out of those things which were written in the books." A bird steps lightly on the beach, passes on, and vanishes. But the impress of its foot is hardened into the rock, and long years after it tells the story. Like that impression in nature is the deeper and more permanent impression memory produces in the conscious personality of life and thought for all the future. "And the books were opened." What is that but the opening of the record we ourselves have kept? Every man becomes suddenly aware that the sphere is small. He and God in this matter have been at one. All the record of his life appears within him— his very self, pronouncing in advance the decision of the great Judge. "I saw the dead, small and great, stand before God." It is to be a day of sentence as well as of inquiry. Each heart is to present the record of itself to its Maker.

The older we grow the more conscious we become of the solitariness of life. In early life we are all together, a crowd of children playing in the streets; but as the years go by we detach ourselves, we become individual. We are solitary men and women because we are, each one, the architects of our own character; and as such at last we are to stand before God.

As we advance in this personal experience our lives become also more complex and intricate. It is harder for us to understand our own motives and feelings; and when any one pronounces judgment upon us we resent it. We say, "I do not know myself, and what right have you to pretend to comprehend my motives?" Until at last we are constrained to cry out upon ourselves, "Is it I?"

But we shall each stand before God! "Thou

God seest me." "Thou understandest my thought afar off. Thou compassest my path and my lying down, and art acquainted with all my ways." So that day is to be the revelation of every man to himself, in all that we know of ourselves and do not speak, and in all that we might have known and did not realize, and in all that lies beyond our sight, but is known to Him who looketh not upon the outward appearance, but on the heart.

Now one verse more. Turn to Paul's second letter to the Corinthians, the fifth chapter and the tenth verse, and you will see how it fits exactly into what already has been said. "For we must all appear before the judgment-seat of Christ; that every one may receive the things done in his body, according to that he hath done, whether it be good or bad." The judgment-seat of God is the judgment-seat of the Saviour Jesus Christ. The question, then, that will gather up all others as the books are opened will be put by the Saviour himself: "How have you lived toward me? I gave my life for you; what hast thou done for me?" It will not be what we have thought of ourselves or what others may have thought of us. It will be simply whether we have known Jesus Christ, have opened our hearts to his love, and lived lives that were a tribute of praise to him.

A short time ago, while conversing with one

who desired to unite with the church, she said,
" I want to join the church because I want to do
what is right, and I would like to be better than
I am." I replied, " So far is well; but how about
the Lord Jesus Christ? Do you know him as
your Saviour? Is it your purpose to give yourself to him?" And as promptly as her first
statement, but with inexpressible sadness, came
the answer: " Oh, if that is what it means to be
a Christian, then I am not a Christian." The
struggle of the next two days and the final glad
surrender showed how wide the distinction is
between the self-righteousness of trying to make
ourselves better and the penitent acceptance of
the new life fully offered to us in Him who died
that we might live. "We must all appear before
the judgment-seat of Christ."

Now we know why it is that in that day the
righteous shall shine as the sun in their Heavenly
Father's realm. The joy on their heads shall be
eternal, and sorrow and sighing shall flee away.
For the judgment is to be the day for the
crowning of the work of the Saviour. He came
to seek and to save that which was lost, and in that
day he will present to the Father the " great multitude, which no man can number, of all nations,
and kindreds, and people, and tongues "; all of
whom, without exception, have the one qualifica-
tion for acceptance, that they have heard his voice

and have followed him. Turning again to the Revelation we read: " The books were opened: and another book was opened, which is the book of life." It is the book in which the names are written of those who have loved him. It is the record of new-born souls who have entered into life through him whose name is written on their foreheads, and who has their names written on his heart.

"If any man sin," said this same Apostle John after there had been given him this wonderful revelation—" If any man sin, we have an advocate with the Father, Jesus Christ the righteous "—one who has gone above, and stands waiting for that last day and for our coming. We sinners—you and I and every one of us —have him for Intercessor and Friend; therefore, if any man would meet that day without fear, if any man would be ready for that once-for-all event, the way of preparation is so plain that the wayfaring man need not err therein.

It is simply to believe on the Lord Jesus Christ, it is simply to commit unto him the keeping of your soul, and you shall live in joyful anticipation of that day which is to be the golden day of the crowning of the Son of God, of the perfecting of his work, and of fullness of joy for all who have heard his voice and have loved and trusted and followed him.